Printing Projects Made Fun & Easy

ISBN 0-13-140411-3

92499

hp official guides

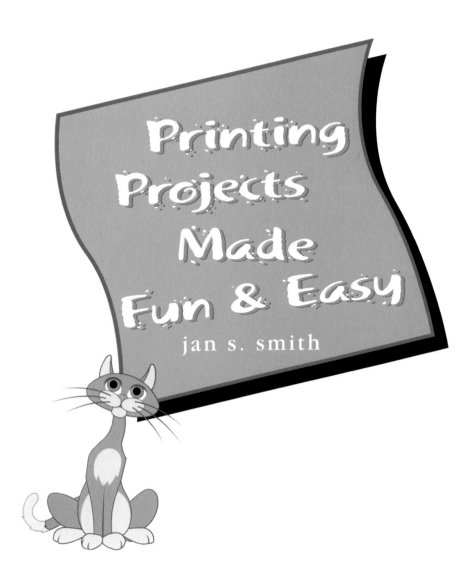

Printing Projects Made Fun & Easy

jan s. smith

the official hp guide

PRENTICE
HALL
PTR

Prentice Hall PTR   Upper Saddle River, NJ 07458   www.phptr.com

Library of Congress Cataloging-in-Publication Data

A CIP catalog record for this book can be obtained from the Library of Congress.

Editorial/production supervision: *Patti Guerrieri*
Composition: *BLW + Associates*
Cover design director: *Jerry Votta*
Cover design: *Talar Boorujy*
Cover photography: *Rose Studios*
Manufacturing manager: *Alexis R. Heydt-Long*
Executive editor: *Jill Harry*
Editorial assistant: *Kate Wolf*
Marketing manager: *Dan DePasquale*
Publisher, Hewlett-Packard Books: *Patricia Pekary*

© 2003 Hewlett-Packard Company

Published by Pearson Education, Inc.
Publishing as Prentice Hall PTR
Upper Saddle River, New Jersey 07458

Prentice Hall books are widely used by corporations and government agencies for training, marketing, and resale. For information regarding corporate and government bulk discounts, please contact: Corporate and Government Sales (800) 382-3419 or corpsales@pearsontechgroup.com.

Printed in the United States of America

10   9   8   7   6   5   4   3   2   1

ISBN 0-13-140411-3

Pearson Education LTD.
Pearson Education Australia PTY, Limited
Pearson Education Singapore, Pte. Ltd.
Pearson Education North Asia Ltd.
Pearson Education Canada, Ltd.
Pearson Educación de Mexico, S.A. de C.V.
Pearson Education—Japan
Pearson Education Malaysia, Pte. Ltd.

To my wonderful husband,
Tom,
and our terrific son,
Jake.

Table of Contents

Foreword

Welcome to one of the most exciting books and CDs around!

At HP, we delight our customers with great imaging and printing products. Now it is our pleasure to share with you some of our customers' favorite printing projects. Author Jan Smith is a long-term HP employee who has personally completed each of these projects. I trust that you'll have great fun and be pleasantly surprised at just how easy these printing ideas are to create, thanks to HP products and Jan's terrific how-to advice.

So enjoy Jan's engaging book. You'll find it to be great fun.

Happy reading and printing!

Vyomesh Joshi
Executive Vice President
Imaging & Printing Group
Hewlett-Packard Company

Acknowledgments

A lot of wonderful—and wonderfully creative—people helped bring this book and CD into your home.

I'd like to thank a small but enormously talented group of artists, designers, illustrators, and animators, including Loren Weeks, Maiken Kling, Melissa Seifer, John Burton, Dan Mandish, Joel Mandish, Tim Larson, Kaci Kyler, Pamela Standley, Sean Fitzgerald, Danny Rubyono, and Tom Lakovic. Together, they helped bring much life and color and playfulness into this book and CD.

I would also like to express my sincere appreciation to Susan Rowe, Frank Rogers-Witte, and Vyomesh Joshi for encouraging me to follow my passion for printing. They've been just great!

For sheer inspiration, I looked to the fantastic Printsville team at HP. For years, they've been making the most awesome printing projects! And for all sorts of other great project ideas, I tapped into the skills of Jennifer Commons, Chad Summervill, Amy Kelm, Chris Morgan, Stacy Jones, Grace Harvester, Jill Kramer, Christi Putz, and Angela Wo.

Heartfelt thanks to my dear neighbors and friends, the Burkes, the Emerys, and the Wises, who make every day a day for joyous celebration! I've loved making all sorts of family calendars, banners, cards, and other arts and crafts projects with them.

And, as always, I want to thank Pat Pekary, who manages our HP Press, and Jill Harry, my Prentice Hall editor. They each provided terrific guidance and good cheer along the way.

About the Author

Jan S. Smith is a senior communications specialist for the Imaging & Printing Group at Hewlett-Packard Company. In that role, she has produced dozens of award-winning multimedia videos, films, CDs, and television programs. Jan has worked for HP for 14 years. Before joining HP, she was a college professor for 11 years, teaching communications courses. Jan has a Bachelor of Arts degree in political science from the University of California, a Masters degree in journalism and advertising from the University of Oregon, and a Ph.D. in telecommunications from the University of Oregon. Jan is a mom and a wife, and loves to make all sorts of artsy-craftsy things using her home printer.

Introduction

I get the biggest kick out of making things with my printer—especially when the instructions are easy and the results look super snazzy!

Now you can experience all the same joys of printing. Just flip through the pages of *Printing Projects Made Fun & Easy*. Pick a great-looking project, pop in your CD, and follow the intuitive menu of options.

In a matter of moments, you'll be making all sorts of goodies that will bring smiles to the faces of your family members and friends. You'll be beaming with delight!

The CD is organized just like the book. On the home page, you will see five icons (each correlating to the five chapters in the book). If you click on one of these icons, a submenu of the different sections you can go to appears. From there you can go to a new page showing all the projects within that section. Once you find the project you want and choose the design, go ahead and print. And in case you get lost or aren't sure what to do next, there are hints along the bottom bar for extra help.

The project and instruction files are all printable Adobe pdf files. Adobe pdf file is a universal format—with all fonts, formatting, graphics, and color embedded into one nice, easy-to-use file. Some of the project pdf files on the CD are editable, so you can click, highlight, and type to customize them just for you. It's incredibly simple, lightning fast, and so much fun to use. If you are interested in learning more about Adobe® Acrobat® or have any other questions, there is free online support from Adobe; just visit: *http://www.adobe.com/support/readguide.html*.

Share some happiness! Share some color! Share some love!

With *Printing Projects Made Fun & Easy,* getting there is half the fun.

Choosing the Right Paper and Ink for Printing

How to Select Paper

It's easy not to think about paper—just borrow what's in the copier machine, right? But if you've seen the difference that a quality paper makes—especially one designed specifically for your printer—you also know it's hard to go back to copier paper for anything but the most ordinary of documents. Paper designed for your printer looks and performs better every time.

Using special printer paper will not only give you better results, it will also be less costly: You'll have fewer paper jams, and your output will look great every time. But there's more to plain white paper than meets the eye. Here are the basics of using and selecting paper for general use and printing photos.

A Crash Course in Paper Basics

First take into account what you'll be printing. Black-and-white documents are quite different from full-color photos. Some papers are multipurpose and therefore good for both; but if you want crisp, vibrant photos that will last a long time, you should use paper that's designed just for photos.

If you're looking for good general-use paper, think about the following:

- *Weight.* Paper weight ranges from lightweight newsprint to very heavy cardboard. Most quality business paper is 20- to 24-pound (lb) bond, with greeting card papers at the heavier end of the scale, usually in the range of 60- to 65-lb cardstocks. Metric equivalents are expressed in grams per square meter, abbreviated as g/m2.

- *Thickness.* The thickness of a paper affects its handling and is most applicable to photo papers. Generally, thicker media will be stiffer and will resist creases and tears. Thickness is most often expressed as a unit of measure called a *mil*.

- *Brightness.* A higher brightness value means that more light is reflected from the surface of the paper, providing crisper text with better contrast and a brighter background for color and images. HP's brightest papers include Bright White for inkjet printing and Premium Choice for laser printing.

- *Finish.* Finishes for laser and inkjet papers are becoming increasingly sophisticated, with numerous choices for a variety of applications. They range from matte to glossy, with lessening degrees of glossiness, sometimes described as semigloss, soft-gloss, or satin-gloss. Many people prefer the mirror-like finish of high-gloss media for color photographs, and smooth matte finishes for black-and-white photographs and business documents. (Be careful with extremely smooth, shiny, or coated papers that aren't specifically designed for your printer. They can cause jams and even repel ink.)

- *Opacity.* Opacity describes how well the paper blocks the passage of light through it. Highly opaque media prevent print from showing through to the other side and are considered good for printing on both sides —for example, for brochures, newsletters, calendars, and other similar applications.

Here's what to look for in paper for printing photos:

- *Whiteness.* For photo or picture printing, keep in mind that whiter papers produce sharper, more vibrant colors. Ink is translucent. Light passes through it and bounces off the paper, then passes back through the ink. The paper color therefore affects the color you see when you print.
- *Thickness.* Some photo projects—like calendars—require a heavier paper stock. But if it's too thick, it could jam up your printer.
- *Surface.* For printouts with crisp lines and intense, high-quality colors, the surface of the paper is key. Glossy paper produces vibrant color but is susceptible to fingerprints, so matte paper might be a better choice for prints that will be handled often.

Your best bet is to buy a paper sampler with various weights and finishes. That way, you can see for yourself what kind of results you get.

Specialty Paper for Printing

Remember the old days when computer paper came in long, continuous sheets? You had to thread it carefully through the printer, making sure the holes along the edges were caught properly by the tractor feet. Then you faced the time-consuming task of pulling off those perforated edges and manually separating each page from the next.

Paper has come a long way in the past two decades. Just about every mainstream printing device today uses some kind of plain bond paper in easy-loading paper trays, though there's nothing plain about the variety of specialty papers currently available for printers. A wide range is available to suit the needs of any and every computer user.

You can also save money by using the new specialty papers to print all sorts of things that you used to have to take to a professional printer. (Of course, before you start experimenting, be sure to check in your printer manual for paper compatibility.) Here's a rundown on papers that will fire your creativity.

Photo paper: Akin to paper used by film developers, photo paper is specifically designed to produce high-quality, color-rich images that are hard to distinguish from traditionally developed photographs. Most of HP's photo papers come in a choice of matte or glossy finishes and a variety of print sizes, including convenient 4 x 6 for affordable everyday prints and large portrait-size papers for studio-quality enlargements.

Greeting cards: Paper designed specifically for greeting cards is thicker, prescored (folded), and smaller than regular paper. You can personalize the cards with your own text and images. HP greeting card papers come in a variety of sizes, colors, and finishes—including linen in white and ivory—with matching envelopes. HP also has a card studio with free templates that let you create your own greeting cards in a snap.

Glossy paper: Glossy paper produces vibrant color but is susceptible to fingerprints. This paper has a shiny, coated surface on one or both sides and is ideal when you need a polished printout. For brochures, flyers, report covers, and special presentations, glossy papers produce colorful images and crisp text equal to professional printing. HP's line of brochure and flyer paper comes in a range of sizes to meet all of your printing needs.

Transparencies: These clear sheets of plastic are used with overhead projectors for presentations.

Stickers and labels: Stickers and labels are available for mail, folders, diskettes, CDs, and whatever else you can think of. You can use fonts, images, and colors to customize them. Restickables allow for even more creative flexibility.

Craft papers: Specialty papers offer a wide range of possibilities to the craftsperson. HP's iron-on transfers make it easy to make your own T-shirts, photo pillows, and much more. Or get your message out loud and clear with HP banner paper. Also available are craft papers specially formulated for printers, such as vellum and parchment, printable sheets of fabric-like felt and canvas, printable Mylar, shrink-wrap plastic, and window clings, making the world of printing practically limitless.

Again, remember to check for compatibility with your printer when you use specialty papers. Not doing so can lead to paper jams and other problems.

Ink and Toner Basics
You use them every day, but you probably don't think about them until they inconveniently run out in the middle of a large print job. Yes, we're talking about ink and toner. Whether you're printing straight black-and-white text or high-color photos, it's important to know that all inks are not created equal.

Inkjet Ink
To understand why some inks work better with your printer than others, it's necessary to understand a little bit about how ink is made. Traditional inks—like those used in your nice ballpoint pen—are oil-based and use dyes made of minuscule suspended particles for colorants. Using oil-based inks in a printer, however, can lead to trying maintenance problems, so instead most inkjet printers use

water-based inks. Unfortunately, in earlier inkjet printers, water-based inks would often bleed, smear, and run, particularly if the printed page was not allowed to dry properly or if it were to get wet.

In recent years, the chemistry of inks has improved considerably as manufacturers have developed ways to improve the vibrancy, clarity, and longevity of the printed product. Ink additives are used in varying amounts to control things like saturation, drying time, and resistance to fading.

But the improvements do not lie entirely in the ink. Preconditioned papers can help improve inkjet printing because they are primed with an agent that helps bind the ink to the paper, reducing smearing and bleeding. When manufacturers recommend using only their ink and paper in your printer, it's not because they want to hold a monopoly on your purchases. It is because the three components—printer, ink, and paper—have been designed to work together to reach the most satisfactory results possible.

Laser Printer Toner
Unlike inkjet printers, laser printers use toner, a dry, powdery substance that is adhered to the paper using an electronic charge. It is specially designed to melt very quickly, and a component of wax makes the toner more  amenable to the process that fuses the toner to the paper. Monochrome printers use a single cartridge of black toner. Color models use four cartridges, one each of cyan, magenta, yellow, and black.

Like ink for inkjet printers, it is always best to use the toner recommended by the manufacturer, because the inner workings of the machine are designed to work with toner of a particular consistency and particle size. Using a different, lower-grade toner can result in smeared print outs (if the drum inside the printer isn't cleaned properly) or lead to jams and other internal problems.

Ink and Toner Refills
The temptation to purchase third-party cartridges or generic refills for your inkjet or laser printer can be strong, especially when the budget is tight. But in the end, the little bit you save in money will be lost in the quality of your end result. By following manufacturer recommendations, you can be sure you're getting the best out of your printer.

For fast, easy, online shopping for all of your inkjet and laser printing needs, come and visit *hpshopping.com*.

Chapter 1

HOME & FAMILY

Take a delightfully creative journey
in and around your home. You'll find
everything here but the kitchen sink!

Around the House

Home Sweet Home! Make it even sweeter with these delightful printing projects!

Canning Kit

When you want your jar toppers, labels, and tags to look as delicious as the yummy foods you're craving, try printing these. You'll be berry glad you did!

Project 1: Jar Topper

A wonderful way to top off your hard work.

Materials Needed:

HP Bright White Inkjet paper

Scissors

Ribbon or raffia

Instructions:

1. Choose design and print pdf file.
2. Cut out paper topper along dotted line.
3. Place topper over jar.
4. Tie a piece of coordinating ribbon or raffia around jar lid to secure the piece of paper to lid.

Project 2: Tags

A beautiful card for the chef to sign.

 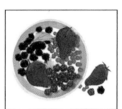

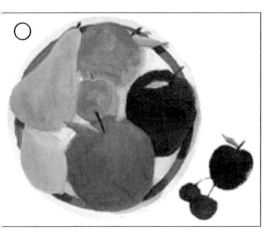

Materials Needed:

HP Card or Cover stock

Cutting mat, metal ruler, and X-ACTO knife

Hole punch

Instructions:

1. Choose design and print pdf file.

2. Trim where indicated.

3. Fold in half and punch where indicated.

4. Tie to raffia or ribbon on jar topper.

Project 3: Jar Labels

Add a splash of color to your preserves.

 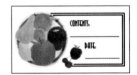

 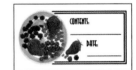

Materials Needed:

Full Sheet White Label stock

Cutting mat, metal ruler, and X-ACTO knife

Instructions:

1. Choose design and print pdf file.

2. Trim labels and fill in information.

3. Apply to jar and enjoy!

Note: Check your printer specifications on how to load special media such as label stock.

Project 4: Gift Labels

From your kitchen.

Materials Needed:

Full Sheet White Label stock

Cutting mat, metal ruler, and X-ACTO knife

Instructions:

1. Choose design and print pdf file.
2. Write your name, trim labels, and apply to jar.
3. Give to friends and family.

Note: Check your printer specifications on how to load special media such as label stock.

Multimedia

When you want your videocassettes, audiocassettes, and CD-ROMs to look as colorful and professional as what you have on them, try one of these projects.

Project 1: CD Covers and Inserts

So easy to make.

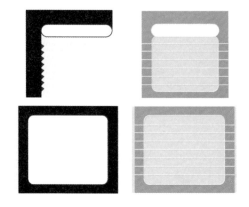

Materials Needed:

HP Inkjet Bright White paper

Cutting mat, metal ruler, and X-ACTO knife

Instructions:

1. Print pdf file.
2. Follow instructions on pdf file for trimming and folding.
3. Put into jewel case and enjoy.

Project 2: Audiocassette Case Covers

Mix and match to clearly identify your tapes.

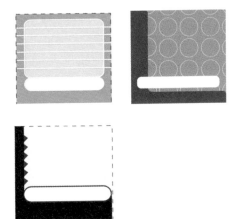

Materials Needed:

Full Sheet White Label stock

Cutting mat, metal ruler, and X-ACTO knife

Instructions:

1. Print pdf file.

2. Trim and fold where indicated.

3. Apply label to outside of cassette case.

Note: Check your printer specifications on how to load special media such as label stock.

Project 3: Audiocassette Face Labels

The finishing touch.

Materials Needed:

Full Sheet White Label stock

Cutting mat, metal ruler, and X-ACTO knife

Instructions:

1. Print pdf file.
2. Trim face labels.
3. Apply label to cassette face.

Note: Check your printer specifications on how to load special media such as label stock.

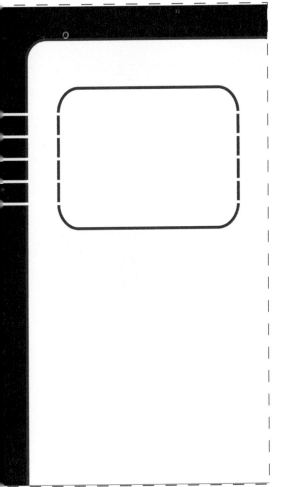

Project 4: Videocassette Case Covers

Organize your video library in no time.

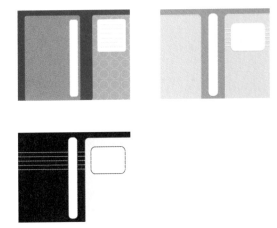

Materials Needed:

Full Sheet White Label stock

Cutting mat, metal ruler, and X-ACTO knife

Instructions:

1. Print pdf file.
2. Trim and fold where indicated.
3. Apply label to outside of cassette sleeve or in between clear cover and case.

Note: Check your printer specifications on how to load special media such as label stock.

Project 5: Videocassette Face and Spine Labels

Cross your t's and dot your i's.

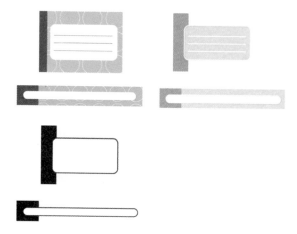

Materials Needed:

Full Sheet White Label stock

Cutting mat, metal ruler, and X-ACTO knife

Instructions:

1. Print pdf files from CD.

2. Trim out labels on cutting mat.

In the Garden

Everything's coming up roses, veggies, and cute little scarecrows when you let your imagination loose with these treats from the garden!

Project 1: Seed Packets

Now you can package your specialty seeds.

Materials Needed:

HP Bright White Inkjet paper

Cutting mat, metal ruler, and X-ACTO knife

Glue stick or double-sided tape

Instructions:

1. Print pdf file from CD.
2. Follow trim and folding instructions on pdf.
3. Tape or glue where indicated.
4. Share your crop with friends and family.

Project 2: Iron-Ons

Make a special gift for a gardener you know.

Materials Needed:

HP Inkjet Iron-On Transfer material

Scissors and iron

Light colored cotton T-shirt

Instructions:

1. Print pdf onto transfer material (it will be backwards).
2. Cut out design, leaving 1/4" white space.
3. Iron transfer to T-shirt per box instructions.

Warning: Do not use iron-on transfer material with any laser printer or printer that uses heat to fuse the ink. It may melt the material and damage the printer.

Project 3: Garden Tags

No more confusion between plants.

Materials Needed:

HP Card stock or Bright White Inkjet paper

Cutting mat, metal ruler, and X-ACTO knife

Wooden dowels or sticks

Self-laminating sheets (to protect ink)

Instructions:

1. If the pdf contains *Click Here to Edit* or similar instructions, edit the file on screen before printing, otherwise, go to step 2.
2. Print pdf file. Apply self-laminating sheets.
3. Trim tags and attach to sticks.
4. Put in your garden and enjoy!

The Practical Home

Now let's see. First on my list for today: recipes for Mom, shopping for party, and maintenance on the house. So much to do!

Project 1: Herb Theme Recipe Cards

Mmm, yummy...

Materials Needed:

1 or more sheets of HP Card or Cover stock

Cutting mat, metal ruler, and X-ACTO knife

Instructions:

1. If editable: Type your recipe into the space provided on pdf file before you print. Or, delete the sample text and handwrite after.
2. Print the recipe cards onto card stock, and set them aside to dry completely.
3. Place the cutting mat underneath the printed card stock. Using the X-ACTO knife and the ruler as your guide, trim away the white areas from each card.
4. Share your delicious recipes with friends and family.

Note: Put your finished recipe cards in plastic sleeves or laminate them to protect from spills.

Project 2: Handy Lists

Something for almost everything.

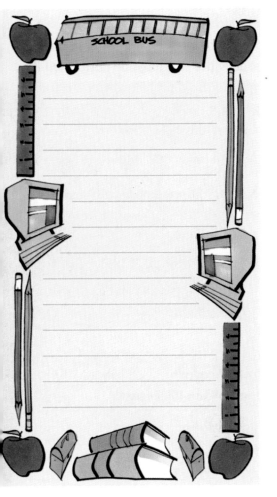

Materials Needed:

HP Bright White Inkjet paper

Cutting mat, metal ruler, and X-ACTO knife

Instructions:

1. Print pdf file. Let dry.

2. Trim out and use.

Note: Not all designs shown. See CD for additional pdf files.

Family Ties

Choose from among these memory makers for your journeys down Memory Lane.

Yesterday and Today

Something old, something new, something borrowed, something blue...

Project 1: 1940s Scrapbook Journal

Nostalgic pages for clippings and photos.

Materials Needed:

9 or more sheets of HP Card or Cover stock

Butter knife or bone folder

Glue stick

Cutting mat, metal ruler, and X-ACTO knife

Ribbon or raffia (24" long)

Clear nail polish

2 to 4 clothespins and hole punch

Clippings, letters, and photos for inside

Instructions:

1. Print artwork from pdf file. Let dry.
2. Follow instructions on CD for scoring and binding journal.

Project 2: 1940s Magnets

Your refrigerator never looked so good.

Materials Needed:

Printable Magnetic Inkjet paper

Cutting mat, metal ruler, and X-ACTO knife

Instructions:

1. Print pdf file on to magnetic paper.

2. Trim magnets and enjoy!

Note: Not all magnets shown. See pdf file on CD for complete designs. Check your printer specifications on how to use and load special media such as magnetic paper.

Project 3: Then and Now Activity Book.

Fun for any generation.

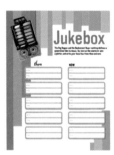

Materials Needed:

6 to 10 sheets of HP Card or Cover stock

Glue stick and felt tip pens

3-hole punch

Instructions:

1. Print all pages of pdf file.
2. Hole punch and put into 3-ring binder, or use other binding suggestions on CD.
3. Fill out, glue photos, and enjoy.

Note: Not all pages shown. See CD for all pdf files.

Project 4: Photo Family Tree

Your photo family tree will be a wonderful centerpiece for your reunion.

Here's a great idea for your next family reunion

- Scan photos of family members into your computer. Use a photo-editing program to clean up old pictures. Remove scratches, repair torn edges, and adjust the colors if needed. Resize and crop photos so they focus on the people.
- Add captions to your photos, identifying the person or people in the image, and include details such as the date of the photo and where the photo was taken.
- Print the photos on photo-quality paper. HP has many to choose from. Trim away excess.
- On a piece of posterboard, draw a diagram of an ancestry chart, showing the various branches of your family. You can even draw or paint the outline of a tree around the chart. Write the family name in large letters at the bottom.
- Using mounting tape, attach the trimmed photos to the tree, starting with the oldest ones at the "trunk" and spreading out through the branches.

- Decorate the borders of the family tree with stickers, stamps, dried leaves and flowers, or family mementos.

More ideas for creative family memories

- Create a digital photo family tree using the collage function of your image editor. You can display this on a Web site, email it to family members, or print it out and frame it.
- Collect family stories from relatives. Using a word processor or desktop publishing software, assemble the stories with your photos and print them out in book form. Add a cover, and give it as a special gift.
- Create a calendar with your photos so that you can remember your family's history throughout the year. Copy houses can spiral bind them, or you can use metal rings to hold the pages together.

Kids and Pets

Purr-fect printing projects for the
little ones in your life!

Kid's Table

When you want your kids to enjoy the dining experience as much as you want to enjoy the dinner, try one of these projects to keep their interest!

Project 1: Double-Sided Kid's Placemat

With so many fun games, your kids won't even have time to play with their food.

Materials Needed:

2 sheets HP Card or Cover stock

Glue stick

Self-laminating sheet

Instructions:

1. Print pdf files.
2. Glue pages back to back.
3. Put between self-laminating sheets to protect ink from spills.

Project 2: Lunch Bags

Package your kids' lunch in style.

Nutrition Facts

Calories 10,986

Total Fat 500g	99%
Sodium 3400mg	99%
Total Carb 800g	100%
Protein 0g	

INGREDIENTS: PIZZA, POTATO CHIPS, SOFT DRINK, CANDY BAR, POPCORN, DONUT.

CONTAINS NO SIGNIFICANT NUTRITIONAL VALUE AND CONSISTS ENTIRELY OF ARTIFICIAL INGREDIENTS.

Materials Needed:

Standard white or brown lunch bag

Instructions:

1. Place a standard lunch bag face down on a piece of 8-1/2" x 11" paper.
2. Tape the top (open) edge of the bag to the top edge of the paper.
3. Insert the bag and paper into the printer with the bag side facing down.
4. Choose design, and print pdf file.
5. Pack a good lunch.

Growing Up

Use this fun wall chart to record your children's growth spurts. Note each child's initials next to the height marks.

Project 1: Giant Giraffe Growth Chart

They grow so fast!

Materials Needed:

HP Bright White Inkjet paper

Self-laminating sheets

Instructions:

1. Print each page of the pdf file. Let dry.
2. Tape ends together to make one tall giraffe.
3. Protect pages with self-laminating sheets, or take the taped-up giraffe to a copy house to have it laminated in one piece.
4. Hang on a wall or back of a door.

Pamper Your Pet

No bones about it—pets deserve the best! Read on for purr-fect ways to say "I love you" with some unique print projects.

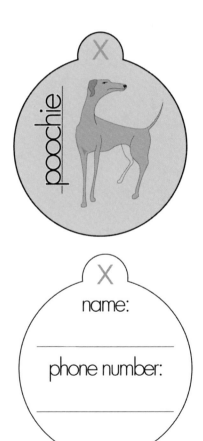

Project 1: Pet Set ID Tags

Keep tabs on your furry friends no matter where they roam.

Materials Needed:

HP Card or Cover stock

Small sheets of laminate

Small split ring

Pen, scissors, and small hole punch

Glue stick

Instructions:

1. Print artwork from pdf file. Let dry.
2. Fill in pet information and trim both sides.
3. Glue front and back together.
4. Laminate the tag per instructions and trim, leaving 1/4" around design.
5. Punch hole where indicated and attach ring.
6. Put on your pet's collar.

Project 2: Pet Set Food Dish Placemats

Spills are easy to clean with these mats.

Materials Needed:

HP Card or Cover stock

Self-laminating sheets

Instructions:

1. Print artwork from pdf file. Let dry.
2. Put between self-laminating sheets to protect ink from spills, or take it to your local copying store to have it laminated.
3. Ring the dinner bell.

Project 3: Pet Set Notecards

These notecards will be happily received by any friend or loved one.

Materials Needed:

HP Card or Cover stock

Scissors

Pen and envelope

Instructions:

1. Print artwork from pdf file. Let dry.

2. Fold and cut out the card where indicated (there will be a 1/2" tab left over to secure the open side).

3. Fill in your good wishes, use a Pet Set Sticker to seal, place in envelope, and send to a friend.

Note: Above thumbnails show card fronts only.

Project 4: Pet Set Stickers

Accessorize anything with these darlings.

Materials Needed:

Full Sheet White Sticker paper

Scissors

Instructions:

1. Print artwork from pdf file. Let dry.
2. Cut out the stickers where indicated.

Project 5: New Pet Announcements

Notify everyone about a new arrival.

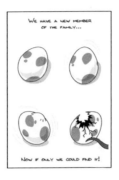

Materials Needed:

HP Card or Cover stock

Scissors

Pen and envelope

Instructions:

1. Print artwork from pdf file. Let dry.
2. Fold on center line and trim out cards where indicated.
3. Fill in your new pet's information and send.

Chapter 2

PHOTO FUN & CRAFTS

Taking pictures is always fun. Turning those pictures into keepsakes is magical!

Photo Projects

Print it, frame it, and glow with joy!

Memorabilia

You've taken beautiful pictures. Now what do you put them in? Use these projects and create real masterpieces.

Project 1: Photo Frames

Want to print your own frame? No problem!

Materials Needed:

HP Card stock or Printable Magnetic sheets

Cutting mat, metal ruler, and X-ACTO knife

Photo

Instructions:

1. Print pdf file onto desired paper. Let dry.
2. Trim white areas away from the frame, including the picture window.
3. If on card stock, tape photo to the back. If on magnetic paper, put your photo behind the frame and attach it to any metal surface.

Project 2: Mailable Photo Frames

A great surprise to find in the mailbox!

fold and tape ends together to create a stand

Materials Needed:

3 sheets of HP Card or Cover stock

Cutting mat, metal ruler, and X-ACTO knife

1 Full Sheet White Label stock

Double-sided tape

Butter knife or scoring tool

Spoon

Scissors and photos

Instructions:

1. Customize the photo frame by typing addresses where indicated, or delete to have a blank field.
2. Print pages 1 to 3 of the pdf onto card stock. Let dry.
3. Trim white areas away from each page.
4. See CD for complete assembly instructions, including scoring, folding, and taping tabs.
5. Print page 4 of the pdf file onto clear sticker paper. Let dry. Refer to CD for application.

Project 3: Photo Brag Book

Whether it's a trip to Tahiti, Junior's big recital, or your honeymoon, you've got plenty to boast about!

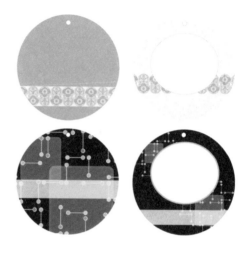

Materials Needed:

3 or more sheets HP Card or Cover stock

Cutting mat, metal ruler, and X-ACTO knife

Double-sided tape

Butter knife or scoring tool and spoon

Hole punch and scissors

Screw post or ribbon for binding

Photos

Self-laminating sheets (optional)

Instructions:

1. Customize the book cover (pg. 1) by typing your message in space provided. Or, select and delete for a blank field.

2. Print cover on card stock. Let dry.

3. Customize photo page (pg. 2) as above.

4. Print photo page on card stock. Let dry.

Project 3: Photo Brag Book

Instructions (continued):

5. Repeat steps 3 and 4 for all of your photos.

6. Print out the brag book back cover (pg. 3) on card stock. Let dry.

7. For easier folding, score all pages. See CD for details on how to do this.

8. Fold along scored lines, and crease with the back of a spoon.

9. Trim pieces of lamination to cover the circle on each page of your brag book. (This is optional, but will protect and extend the life of your book.)

10. Peel the backing from each sheet, one at a time, and place on top of the circles. See CD for how to completely seal to paper.

11. Cut the photo window from each of the photo pages.

12. From the back, tape your photos in place.

13. Apply double-sided tape to the back of each brag book circle. Fold each page in half along the crease and press firmly.

14. One at a time, trim white areas away from the circle using the cutting mat and X-ACTO knife.

15. Once all of the circles have been cut, punch out the gray dot at the top of each page.

16. To assemble the book, insert the screw posts through all of the pages and screw them together. If desired, a ribbon can be tied to bind the pages together instead.

Crafts

Have some intergalactic and soulful fun!

Get Inspired

Sometimes an inspiring phrase or the sight of a beautiful flower is all it takes to bring a smile to a friend.

Project 1: Jewelry

Fun, playful, simply dazzling. You go, friend!

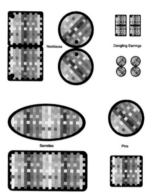

Materials Needed:

HP Bright White Inkjet paper or Card stock

Scissors and glue stick

Barrette backs, pins, earrings, and ribbon

Instructions:

1. Print pdf file. Let dry.
2. Trim away all white areas.
3. Glue pendants back to back and put on cord or ribbon.
4. Glue earrings back to back and put on metal earring hooks.
5. Attach pins and barrettes to back sides of other designs. Have fun!

Project 2: CD Clocks

Here's a colorful clock you can make yourself—and recycle an old CD at the same time!

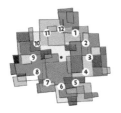 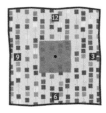

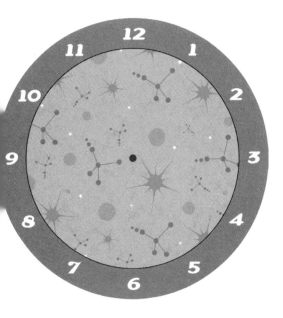

Materials Needed:

HP Card or Cover stock

Cutting mat, metal ruler, and X-ACTO knife

Double-sided tape (high tack)

Used CD

Fishing line and beads (optional for retro)

Clock movement and battery

Instructions:

1. Print pdf file on card stock. Let dry.
2. Trim away all white areas around face.
3. Cut out gray circle in center of clock face for clock movement to go through.
4. Unscrew the clock movement components from the shaft, then attach the CD to the front of the clock movement with double-sided tape. (CD will support clock face.)
5. Apply double-sided tape to the CD front and place clock face on top. Be sure clock face numbers are in position before pressing.
6. Assemble clock movement per instructions.
7. Put in batteries and hang up the clock.

Note: See special instructions on CD for retro clock.

Project 3: Inspirational Art Mousepad

Words of inspiration at your fingertips.

Materials Needed:

HP Inkjet Iron-On Transfer material

Cutting mat, metal ruler, and X-ACTO knife

8" x 10" mousepad (or larger)

Instructions:

1. Print pdf file on iron-on transfer material. (Design will appear backwards.)
2. Trim art, leaving 1/4" white space around design.
3. Center design and follow iron-on transfer instructions from box.

Project 4: Inspirational Art Wallet Cards

Prose in your pocket.

Materials Needed:

HP Bright White Inkjet paper

Cutting mat, metal ruler, and X-ACTO knife

Glue stick

Instructions:

1. Print pdf file. Let dry.
2. Trim where indicated and glue cards back to back. Or, trim outer edges and fold in half.

Project 5: Inspirational Art Notepaper

Beautiful words…beautiful paper.

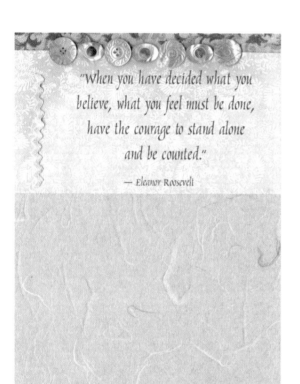

"When you have decided what you believe, what you feel must be done, have the courage to stand alone and be counted."

— Eleanor Roosevelt

Materials Needed:

HP Bright White Inkjet paper

Cutting mat, metal ruler, and X-ACTO knife

Instructions:

1. Print pdf file. Let dry.

2. Cut sheet in half.

3. Enjoy!

Project 6: Inspirational Art Photo Frame

Framed to perfection!

Materials Needed:

HP Bright White Inkjet paper

Cutting mat, metal ruler, and X-ACTO knife

Cardboard

Glue stick

Instructions:

1. Print pdf file. Let dry.

2. Paste entire printout onto cardboard

3. Cut out frame, including photo section.

4. Tape photo to back of frame.

5. To stand frame up, cut a triangle-shaped piece of cardboard and glue to back side.

6. To hang frame, loop a piece of string and tape to back.

Iron-Ons and Textiles

Sew lovely! Sew nice! Sew playful!

Home Sweet Home

Be it ever so humble…

Project 1: Country Kitchen Aprons

The latest fashions for chefs everywhere.

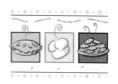 

Materials Needed:

HP Iron-On Transfer material

Scissors

White or light-colored apron

Instructions:

1. Print pdf file onto transfer material. Let dry. (Design will be backwards.)
2. Trim out design, leaving 1/4" white area.
3. Iron your design onto apron per transfer box instructions.

Project 2: Mother's Quilt

There's no one in the world like a mom. She nurtures, protects, and helps us out with homework. She teaches us right from wrong and how to learn from our mistakes. Here's a quilt that celebrates treasured family moments—a gift that will surely warm her heart!

Materials Needed:

HP Iron-On Transfer material

Scanner, digital camera, or digital photos

Sewing machine

12 fabric squares, 10-1/2" x 10-1/2"; use shades of white for photo transfers, solids and prints for a splash of color; 100% cotton or cotton/polyester blend works best on transfers

Fabric fixative and fabric adhesive

Buttons, fabric paints, beads, and ribbon

Instructions:

1. Print your images or art on iron-on transfer paper. (Remember to reverse the image.)
2. Run a bead of fabric fixative on edges of fabric squares. Let dry.
3. Fold under and press all four sides 1/4" (finished size will be 10").
4. Iron your transfer images onto the squares.
5. Organize your design by placing the finished squares on top of the throw (3" from the outer edges). Pin into place.
6. Sew the squares together either by hand or with a sewing machine (a topstitch or zigzag stitch works best.)
7. Add finishing touches to the squares using ribbon, beads, buttons, or fabric paint—get creative and experiment!

Project 3: Dream Pillows

Just the thing to spin sleepy bedtime stories and sweet dreams.

dreamtime

dreamteam

dreammachine

make a wish...

night night

Materials Needed:

HP Iron-On Transfer material

Scissors and iron

Pillow cover or fabric square

Instructions:

1. Print artwork from pdf file onto iron-on transfer material. Let dry.

2. Trim out, leaving 1/4" white space around design. Iron to fabric square or pillow cover per transfer box instructions.

3. If on material square, turn edges under and press all sides. Sew finished transfer fabric square onto pillow.

Note: Not all pillow designs shown. See CD for more.

Special Considerations with Iron-Ons:

1. Warning! Do not use iron-on transfer material with any laser printer or with the HP DeskJet 1200C or HP DeskJet 1600C. The heating elements in these printers can melt the transfer paper and damage the printer. Refer to your printer manual if you are uncertain about yours.

2. For best results, use 100% cotton or cotton/polyester blend fabric.

3. If your fabric is dark colored, use dark iron-on transfer material.

4. Use standard ink when printing your transfer design. Photo and specialty inks are not recommended.

Fuzzy Friends

Fun gift ideas and a moderately challenging sewing project.

Project 1: Beanbag Lizard

Fanciful lizard beanbag for fun!

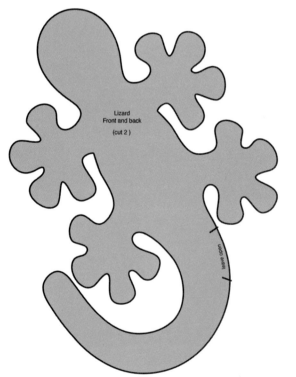

Lizard
Front and back
(cut 2)

leave open

Materials Needed:

HP Bright White Inkjet paper

Fabric (spandex recommended)

Sand or plastic pellets

Needle and thread

Straight pins

Scissors

2 small round black buttons, googly eyes, rhinestones, or fabric paint

Instructions:

1. Print out pattern from pdf file. Let dry.
2. Follow detailed instructions on CD.

Project 2: Beanbag Bunny

Who could resist this soft and loveable bunny!

Materials Needed:

HP Bright White Inkjet paper

12" x 12" piece of white fabric (velour, terry cloth, twill, or nylon recommended)

2" x 12" piece of pink fabric (same as above)

Matching thread

1 1/2" white pom-pom

2 1/4" black pom-poms or small black round buttons

Brown and white embroidery floss

Plastic craft pellets

Fiberfill

Washable fabric glue

Scissors

Sewing machine

Instructions:

1. Print pdf file from CD. Let dry.

2. Follow detailed instructions on CD.

Scrapbooks

Snap, Print, Pop!

Photo Keepsakes

There are unlimited opportunities to share some of life's most treasured moments. Why not turn your memories into creative gifts? They'll be well loved because they come from the heart.

Project 1: Photo Collage

As rewarding to give as they are fun to create.

Materials Needed:

HP Bright White Inkjet paper

10 to 15 photos (depending on frame size)

Cutting mat, metal ruler, and X-ACTO knife

12" x 12" frame (or any size)

Poster board or foam core

Double-sided tape

Scissors (straight-edged or fancy)

Instructions:

1. Choose design and print pdf file.
2. Follow detailed instructions on CD.

Project 2: Graduation and Summer Camp Photo Book

Memory books to capture all the fun!

Materials Needed:

HP Bright White Inkjet paper

Cutting mat, metal ruler, and X-ACTO knife

Pencil and eraser

Acid-free parchment paper

Acid-free photo adhesive

Vellum or other decorative paper

One piece heavy black card stock

Self-adhesive photo corners

Hole punch

1/2 yard of 1" or thicker ribbon

Twenty-four 4" x 6" or smaller photographs

Preparation and Instructions:

1. The finished album will be 9-1/4" x 5". Trim the parchment paper and piece of card stock to those dimensions and set aside.
2. Print one of the pages of this pdf onto either vellum or another sheet of parchment paper. (Vellum will allow the first photograph to show through.) Trim to 9-1/4" x 5".
3. Draw a faint pencil line 1-1/4" from the left-hand sides of your trimmed sheets (the gutter).
4. Punch two holes into the gutter of each piece. They should be 1" from top and bottom, and centered in the gutter. Set the printed cover sheet and card stock aside until you get to step 6.

Project 2: Graduation and Summer Camp Photo Book

Instructions (continued):

5. Place your photographs one by one in the remaining space (8" x 5") of your parchment paper. Make faint pencil marks around each photo to help center it. When the photo is centered, put a small piece of photo adhesive tape on the back of it and press into place. Peel off the backing of four self-adhesive photo corners and attach to the corners of your photo. Repeat this process with the remaining photos and pieces of parchment paper. Be sure to erase any pencil marks you made.

6. Arrange your finished stack of photos in the order you would like them to appear in your book. Place your printed cover sheet on top of the first photograph, using the card stock as the final page. Run a length of ribbon through the holes from front to back. Tie in a bow and trim ends on a diagonal. Apply no-fray fabric solvent or clear nail polish to ribbon edges so they don't fray.

Tip: If you're making multiple copies, you may want to scan your photos into your computer or use digital images rather than work with originals. You can use photo editing software for extra pizzazz.

Project 3: Beach and Camping Scrapbook Kits

Fun, fun, fun!

Materials Needed:

HP Bright White Inkjet paper

Full Sheet White Label stock

Scissors (straight-edged or fancy)

Cutting mat, metal ruler, and X-ACTO knife

Photos, clippings, and memorabilia

Glue stick

Instructions:

1. If the pdf contains *Click Here to Edit* or similar instructions, edit the file on screen before printing, otherwise, go to step 2.
2. Print pdf file. Cut out stickers. Use backgrounds and borders to decorate pages.
3. Add your own photos and clippings.
4. Enjoy!

Chapter 3

SPORTS
& HOBBIES

Hobbyists and sports fans, rejoice!
Score the winning touchdown with
these printable goodies!

Games

I see F*U*N in your future!

Just for Fun

Whether on a road trip or at a family gathering, these games will add some extra fun to the event.

Project 1a: Roadside Americana Trivia Game Envelope

Materials Needed:

2 sheets of HP Card or Cover stock

Cutting mat, metal ruler, and X-ACTO knife

Double-sided tape and glue stick

Butter knife or scoring tool

Instructions:

1. Print pages 2 and 3 on card stock. Let dry.
2. Score the red dotted lines.
3. Cut along the black dotted lines.
4. Cut out the support rectangle and apply glue to one side. Glue the rectangle onto the back of the top part of the envelope.
5. Create windows in the envelope by cutting out the five boxes along the white dotted lines.
6. Fold the envelope flaps (A & B) along the scored lines, and crease. They should be folded away from the front of the envelope.
7. To hold the flaps in place, apply double-sided tape to flaps A & B. Then, fold the back of the envelope (with the map) on top and press firmly to hold in place.

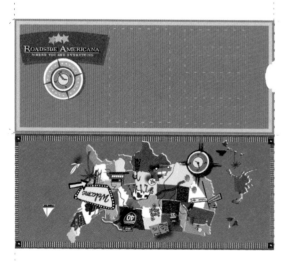

Project 1b: Roadside Americana Trivia Cards

Test your knowledge of the offbeat destinations that make America like no other place on Earth.

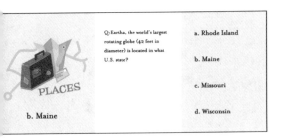

Materials Needed:

6 sheets HP Card or Cover stock

Cutting mat, metal ruler, and X-ACTO knife

Instructions:

1. Print pages 4 to 9 on card stock. Let dry.

2. Trim each card on dotted lines.

3. Slip the cards in the envelope (from Project 1a) and let the trivia challenge begin!

Project 2: American Inventor Trivia Cards

Be inspired by the bright ideas of famous American inventors.

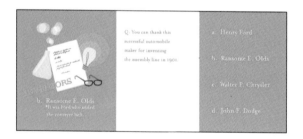

Materials Needed:

6 sheets of HP Card or Cover stock

Cutting mat, metal ruler, and X-ACTO knife

Roadside Americana Trivia Envelope

Instructions:

1. Use the same Roadside Americana Trivia Envelope as you created in Project 1a.
2. Print pages 4 to 9 on card stock. Let dry.
3. Trim each card on dotted lines.
4. Slip the cards in the envelope (from Project 1a) and let the trivia challenge begin!

Project 3: Magic Fortune Teller

Go ahead, ask your burning question…

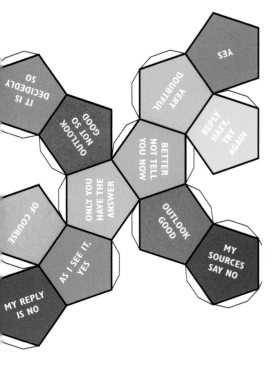

Materials Needed:

HP Card or Cover stock

Cutting mat, metal ruler, and X-ACTO knife

Thin double-sided tape

Instructions:

1. Print pdf file on card stock. Let dry.
2. Trim around outer black lines and fold on all black lines.
3. Apply double-sided tape to each tab to hold the ball together.
4. Ask a question and roll for the answer.

Hobbies

Decorate your garden and yourself!

A Blissful Garden

Happiness is found in the garden. With these colorful projects, your creativity will surely bloom.

Project 1: Gardener's Gear Iron-On Designs

Create garden gear that inspires.

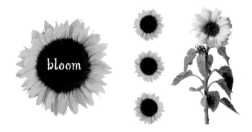

your hands dirty.

Materials Needed:

HP Iron-On Transfer material

Cotton T-shirt, apron, baby onesie, or tote bag

Scissors and iron

Instructions:

1. Choose design and print pdf file. Let dry.
2. Trim around your design, leaving 1/4" white space.
3. Iron on design per transfer instructions.

Project 2: Garden Markers

Descriptive markers ready to grace your garden.

Materials Needed:

HP Card or Cover stock

Cutting mat, metal ruler, and X-ACTO knife

Self-laminating sheets

Wood or plastic plant labels

Instructions:

1. Print desired art from pdf file. Let dry.
2. Place a plant label on the back side of the marker card, pointed end down.
3. Following the laminate directions, sandwich the marker card and plant label together, covering all but the pointy end of the label. Leave enough space between each for trimming. Rub firmly on edges.
4. Cut out each marker, leaving 1/8".

Note: Not all designs shown. See CD for all pdf files.

Project 3: Garden Magnets

Bring a bit of nature into your home.

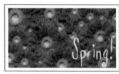

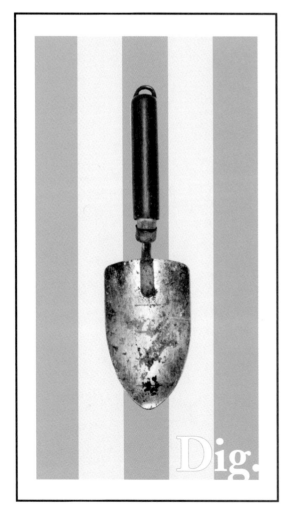

Materials Needed:

Printable Magnetic Inkjet paper

Cutting mat, metal ruler, and X-ACTO knife

Instructions:

1. Print page 2 of pdf file. Let dry.
2. Trim around each image where indicated.

Project 4: Garden Chart and Journal

Keeping track of your buds can be easy and fun!

Materials Needed:

HP Card or Cover stock

Cutting mat, metal ruler, and X-ACTO knife

Double-sided tape

Tape

3 screw posts or ribbon (1/2" wide, 18" long)

Hole punch

Garden photos

Instructions:

1. Print cover from page 2 of pdf file. Let dry. Trim away white areas.

2. Print the garden chart (pg. 3) of pdf file. Print as many copies as you'd like of each. Let dry. Trim away white areas.

3. Print garden photo frame and frame back (pgs. 4–5) of pdf file. Let dry. Trim away white frame windows on all copies.

4. Choose photos and put behind windows in garden photo frame pages. Tape to back.

5. With the garden frame pages face down, apply double-sided tape to the backs.

6. Make sure the frame back art is oriented the same as the frame front. Carefully set the frame backs face up on top of the taped photo frame pages, and press firmly in place.

7. Punch holes in all the journal pages where indicated.

8. Stack the journal pages in order with the cover on top, photo pages on bottom.

9. See CD for detailed assembly and bindery directions.

Sports

Hit a grand slam with your printer!

Baseball Party

Here's the pitch: We've got baseball projects to turn your next game or party into a major league celebration. Every fan in your neighborhood will be sliding into home (yours!).

Project 1: Invitation

It's party time!

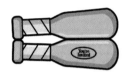

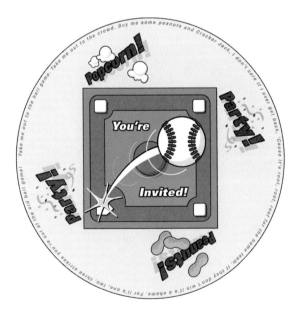

Materials Needed:

HP Card or Cover stock

Cutting mat, metal ruler, and X-ACTO knife

Instructions:

1. Print page 1 of pdf file. Let dry.
2. Turn 180° and place back in printer, printed side face up.
3. Print page 2.
4. Cut around outside of yellow circle.
5. Crease along each of the four sides of the green square to make flaps.
6. Start by folding in one of the flaps and continue around the square. To close, tuck the last flap under the first flap to seal.

Note: See CD for instructions for bat invitation.

Project 2: Magnetic Photo Frames

A great party favor to give away.

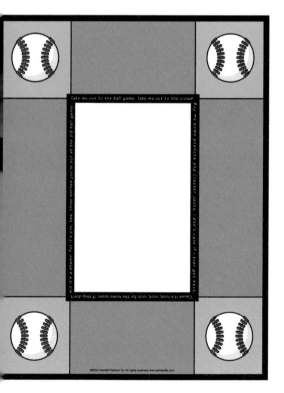

Materials Needed:

Printable Magnetic Inkjet paper

Cutting mat, metal ruler, and X-ACTO knife

Photo

Instructions:

1. Print pdf file on magnetic paper, or print onto HP Bright White Inkjet paper and paste to a magnetic sheet.
2. Cut out all white areas around frame, including interior photo area.
3. Place photo behind magnet and stick frame to a metal surface.

Project 3: Stars Trading Cards

Make everyone at the party a star.

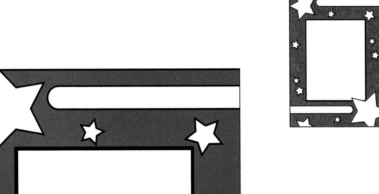

Materials Needed:

HP Card or Cover stock

Cutting mat, metal ruler, and X-ACTO knife

Team photos

Instructions:

1. Type in team name, player name, and number where indicated. Print and let dry.
2. Cut out all white areas around card, including photo window.
3. Tape photo to back of card.

Project 4: Baseball Trading Cards

Make them feel like a pro.

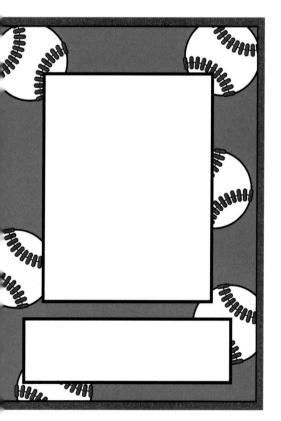

Materials Needed:

HP Card or Cover stock

Cutting mat, metal ruler, and X-ACTO knife

Team photos

Instructions:

1. Type in team name and player's name and position on each card.

2. Cut out all white areas around card, including photo window.

3. Tape photo to back of card.

Project 5: Coasters

Catch those party spills with cool coasters.

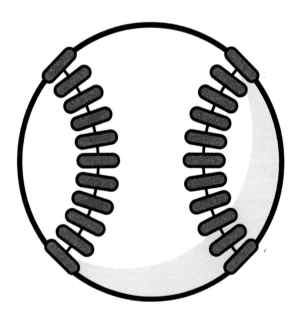

Materials Needed:

HP Bright White Inkjet paper

Scissors and glue stick

Cardboard

Self-laminating sheets

Instructions:

1. Print pdf file. Let dry.

2. Laminate printed sheets to protect ink.

3. Glue to cardboard.

Project 6: Window Cling
Funny when it's fake.

Materials Needed:

Window decals for inkjet printers

Scissors

Instructions:

1. Print pdf file. Let dry.
2. Trim instructions off top and adhere to window.

Warning: Be sure to use materials designed specifically for your printer. To prevent damage, use window decals specifically designed for laser printers or printers that use heat to fuse the ink.

Project 7: Team Roster
Go, team, go!

Materials Needed:

HP Bright White Inkjet paper

Instructions:

1. Type in team name, players' names and stats, and coaches' names.
2. Print pdf file. Let dry.

Project 8: Catcher Game

Super fun and easy game for the party.

Materials Needed:

HP Bright White Inkjet paper

Self-laminating sheet

Instructions:

1. Print pdf file. Let dry.
2. Trim off instructions and laminate sheet.
3. Throw wet cotton balls at the target.
   Closest to the center wins.

Project 9: Score Sheet
And reusable no less!

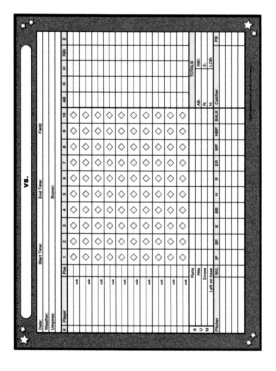

Materials Needed:

HP Bright White Inkjet paper

Self-laminating sheets (optional)

Instructions:

1. Print pdf file. Let dry.
2. If you want to reuse the score sheet, laminate and use removable overhead markers.
3. Keep score.

Project 10: Decorations and Shrinkables

Fun activities for the whole team.

Materials Needed:

White printable shrink sheets for inkjet printers

Scissors

Ribbon or raffia

Instructions:

1. Print pdf on the shrink material. Let dry.
2. Cut out and punch hole in each.
3. Follow instructions for baking that came in the shrink sheet box.

Warning: To prevent damage, be sure to use materials designed specifically for your printer.

Project 11: Thank You Card

A perfect ending to a fun-filled party.

Materials Needed:

HP Card or Cover stock

Scissors

Instructions:

1. Print pdf file. Let dry.
2. Cut out where indicated and fold in half.

Thank You

Soccer Kit

Stay on top of your game with cool soccer projects that coaches, parents, and kids will love. From practical to fun!

Project 1: T-Shirt Iron-On

Mix and match these icons for custom shirts.

Materials Needed:

HP Iron-On Transfer material

Scissors

Iron

Cotton T-shirt

Instructions:

1. Print pdf file onto transfer material. Let dry.
2. Follow iron-on instructions from transfer material box.

Warning: Do not use iron-on transfer material with any laser printer or printer that uses heat to fuse the ink. It may melt the material and damage the printer.

Project 2: Yearbook

Use this scrapbook to capture all the season's highlights. There's room for memories, snapshots, clippings, autographs, and more!

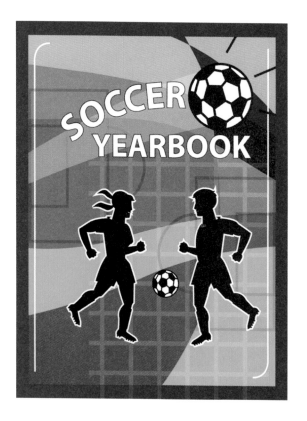

Materials Needed:

6 or more sheets of card stock

Full Sheet White Label stock

Cutting mat, metal ruler, and X-ACTO knife (or scissors)

Double-sided tape

Photos

Pens and markers

Hole punch (optional)

Screw posts, ribbon, three-ring binder, or other binding materials (optional)

Project 2: Yearbook
(continued)

Instructions:

1. Print the yearbook (pgs. 1–6) onto the card stock. Set them aside to dry completely.
2. Place the cutting mat underneath the first page. Using the X-ACTO knife and the ruler as a guide, trim the white areas away from each page.
3. To complete the friends page (pgs. 2–3), cut out the photo.
4. Using the double-sided tape, attach your photos to page 3 where indicated.
5. Apply double-sided tape around the photos on page 3, placing page 2 on top. Press the pages together firmly.
6. Fill in the information under each photo.
7. Print the stickers (pg. 7) onto the label stock. Set them aside to dry completely.
8. Using your pens, photos, and stickers, decorate the pages to create a scrapbook.
9. Decide how you would like to bind your pages and punch holes, if necessary.

Project 3: Editable Soccer Trading Cards

Score big with your team with these cards.

Materials Needed:

HP Bright White Inkjet paper

1 or more sheets of Full Sheet Label stock

1 or more sheets of card stock

Cutting mat, metal ruler, and X-ACTO knife

Player photos (trimmed to 2" x 3-1/4")

Instructions:

1. If the pdf contains *Click Here to Edit* or similar instructions, edit the file on screen before printing, otherwise, go to step 2.
2. Print cards onto label stock. Let dry.
3. Trim out photo windows on each card and roughly cut out the trading card fronts.
4. Peel the paper backing from fronts of the cards and attach to photos.
5. Stick card fronts onto card stock.
6. Trim white areas away from each card.
7. Trim white areas away from card backs.
8. Peel paper backing from backs and apply to the corresponding fronts.
9. Trade cards with your friends and have fun!

Project 4: Editable Soccer Team Roster

Keep track of who's who with this handy tool.

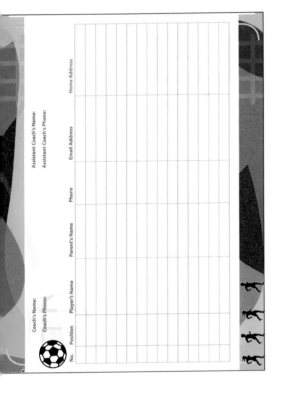

Materials Needed:

HP Bright White Inkjet paper

Instructions:

Edit the pdf file, then print it out. Or, if you'd like to print a blank roster and handwrite the information, highlight the editable text and delete.

Project 5: Editable Certificates

Make one for every player on the team!

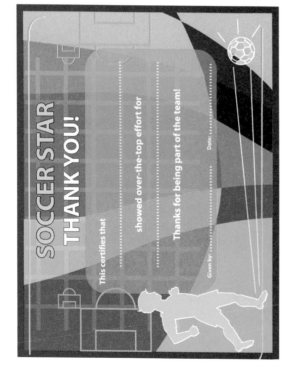

Materials Needed:

HP Bright White Inkjet paper

Instructions:

1. If the pdf contains *Click Here to Edit* or similar instructions, edit the file on screen before printing, otherwise, go to step 2.
2. If you'd like to handwrite your certificates, just highlight the text in the pdf file and delete before printing.
3. Print pdf file. Let dry.

Note: Not all designs shown. There are boy and girl versions of each certificate pdf file on the CD.

The Sports Star

Is there a sports hero in your life? Give her or him some much-deserved credit with a sports-magazine picture frame. You can customize it to include your hero's stats!

Project 1: Sports Magazine Photo Frames

For the "professional" sports stars in your life.

Materials Needed:

Printable Magnetic Inkjet paper or card stock

Cutting mat, metal ruler, and X-ACTO knife

Photo

Instructions:

1. Customize and edit the frame before printing onto magnetic paper. Let dry.
2. Trim the white areas away from the frame, including the picture window.
3. If your frame is printed on card stock, tape your photo in place from the back.
4. If you printed the frame on magnetic paper, put your photo behind the frame and attach it to any suitable metal surface.

Note: See CD for additional frame designs.

Chapter 4

CARDS & STATIONERY

Touch someone's heart with beautiful cards and stationery. Make these treasures right on your home printer!

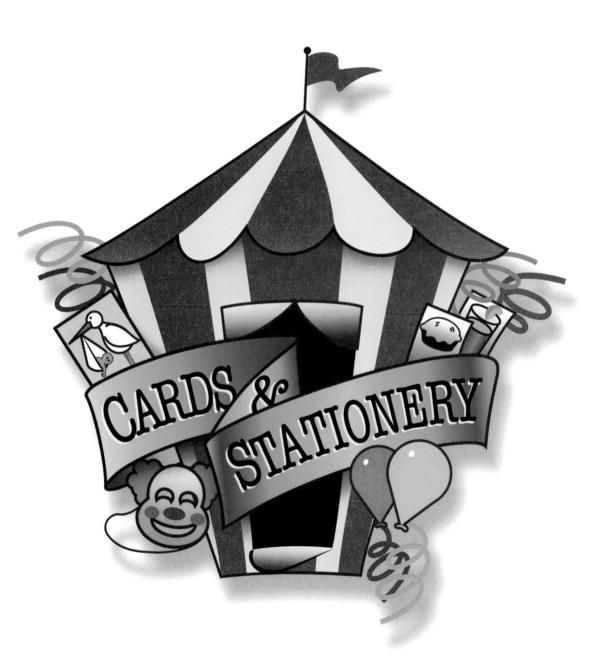

Entertaining

Party on!

Invitations

Get creative and make your own invitations with your home printer. Here are a few of our ideas to get you started.

Project 1: Bridal Shower

I hear bells. Do you hear bells?

Materials Needed:

HP Matte Greeting Cards, 1/4-fold or 1/2-fold

Instructions:

1. If the pdf contains *Click Here to Edit* or similar instructions, edit the file on screen before printing, otherwise, go to step 2.
2. Set your print quality to *Best.*
3. Print a test invitation. If cropping occurs, select *Shrink to Fit,* and print again to ensure sizing.
4. Print your cards onto greeting card paper, and set them aside to dry completely.
5. Finish up by folding the cards in quarters or in half, depending on the layout.

Project 2: Baby Shower

First comes love, then comes marriage, then comes a baby in a baby carriage.

Materials Needed:

HP Matte Greeting Cards, 1/4-fold or 1/2-fold

Instructions:

1. If the pdf contains *Click Here to Edit* or similar instructions, edit the file on screen before printing, otherwise, go to step 2.
2. Set your print quality to *Best*.
3. Print a test invitation. If cropping occurs, select *Shrink to Fit*, and print again to ensure sizing.
4. Print your cards onto greeting card paper, and set them aside to dry completely.
5. Finish up by folding the cards in quarters or in half, depending on the layout.

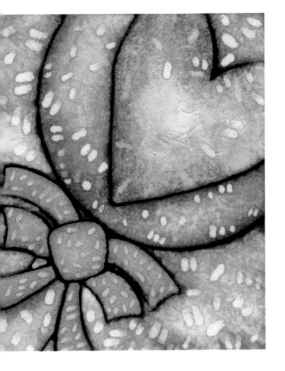

Project 3: Kids' Party

The fun begins long before the party starts with these playful invites.

Note: See CD for pop-up invitation instructions.

Materials Needed:

HP Greeting Card paper, 1/4-fold or 1/2-fold

Instructions:

1. If the pdf contains *Click Here to Edit* or similar instructions, edit the file on screen before printing, otherwise, go to step 2.
2. Print a test of page 1. If cropping occurs, select *Shrink to Fit*, and print again to ensure sizing.
3. Print page 1 onto greeting-card paper, and leave it in the printer tray to dry.
4. Remove the printed page from the printer tray and, without turning the page over, return it to the loading tray.
5. Print page 2 and finish with a fold.

CHAPTER **4** CARDS & STATIONERY / Entertaining

Baby Shower Party Kit

Fun games to play, guest lists and gift lists to keep you organized, and thank you notes to send afterwards. Oh baby!

Project 1: Memory Game
An easy and fun game for the group.

Materials Needed:

HP Bright White Inkjet paper

Pen

Instructions:

1. Print as many copies of the pdf file as needed. Let dry.
2. Instructions for game are at the top of the page. Enjoy!

Project 2: Unscramble the Word Game

Alphabet soup!

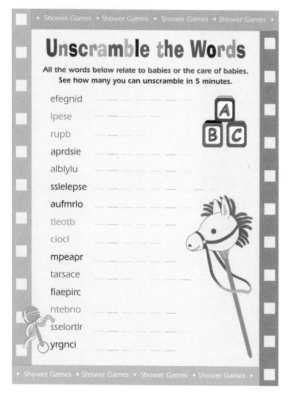

Materials Needed:

HP Bright White Inkjet paper

Pen

Instructions:

1. Print as many copies of the pdf file as needed. Let dry.
2. Instructions for game are at the top of the page. Enjoy!

Project 3: Guest List

Who's coming? Use this to keep track.

Materials Needed:

HP Bright White Inkjet paper

Pen

Instructions:

1. Print pdf file. Let dry.

2. Keep yourself organized and stress-free!

Project 4: Gift List

Organization help for the mom-to-be.

Materials Needed:

HP Bright White Inkjet paper

Pen

Instructions:

1. Print pdf file. Let dry.

2. Write in all the gifts received at the baby shower.

Project 5: Thank You Cards

A perfect ending…

Materials Needed:

HP Greeting Cards, 1/4-fold

Instructions:

1. Print a test card. If cropping occurs, select *Shrink to Fit*, and print again to ensure sizing.
2. Print your cards onto greeting-card paper, and set aside to dry completely.
3. Finish up by folding the cards in quarters.

Fiesta Party Kit

Celebrate with a Mexican flair. This party kit includes everything you'll need for a great fiesta!

Project 1: Editable Invitations

Click, type, and print. As easy as flan.

Materials Needed:

HP Matte Greeting Card paper, 1/4-fold

Instructions:

1. If the pdf contains *Click Here to Edit* or similar instructions, edit the file on screen before printing, otherwise, go to step 2.
2. Set your print quality to *Best*.
3. Print a test invitation. If cropping occurs, select *Shrink to Fit*, and print again to ensure sizing.
4. Print your cards onto greeting-card paper, and set them aside to dry completely.
5. Finish up by folding the cards in quarters.

Project 2: 3D Centerpiece

Spice up the table with this decoration.

Materials Needed:

3 sheets HP Card or Cover stock

Scissors

Glue and double-sided tape

Instructions:

1. Print the centerpiece pdf onto three pieces of card stock. Set them aside to dry.
2. Cut out the pieces along the border.
3. Glue the front and back pieces of the cactus together.
4. Fold each triangular edge of the base piece up and together to form a pyramid.
5. Use the double-sided tape on the tabs of the base to hold the pyramid shape together.
6. Slide the cactus into the slit at the top of the pyramid.

Project 3: Editable Menu Cards

What's for dinner?

Materials Needed:

1 or more sheets HP Card or Cover stock

Cutting mat, metal ruler, and X-ACTO knife

Instructions:

1. Edit the menu cards on screen before printing. The type will repeat itself automatically in the second card.
2. Print the menu cards onto card stock, and set them aside to dry completely.
3. Trim away the white areas from each card.
4. Place a menu card at each table setting.

Project 4: Editable Place Cards

Fun and formal!

Materials Needed:

1 or more sheets HP Card or Cover stock

Cutting mat, metal ruler, and X-ACTO knife

Butter knife or scoring tool, spoon

Instructions:

1. Edit the cards on screen before printing.
2. Print the place cards onto card stock. Print one card for each guest, and set them aside to dry completely.
3. Score the cards with moderate pressure using the butter knife or scoring tool.
4. Trim away the white areas from each card.
5. With each place card face down, fold carefully along the scored edge. Crease the fold firmly with the back of a spoon.
6. Stand a place card at each person's plate.

Project 5: Editable Table Tents

A fun and easy decoration for the table.

Materials Needed:

1 or more sheets HP Card or Cover stock

Cutting mat, metal ruler, and X-ACTO knife

Butter knife or scoring tool, spoon

Instructions:

1. Customize the table tents by typing your guests' names into the space provided. Or, to create a blank field, click on the text section to select it and then press delete.
2. Print the table tents on the card stock. Print as many as you need. There are four table tents per sheet. Let dry completely.
3. For easier folding, score the cards with moderate pressure using the butter knife or scoring tool.
4. Trim the white areas away from all the table tent pages.
5. With each place card face down, fold carefully along the scored edge. Crease the fold firmly with the back of a spoon.

Project 6: Fiesta Candle Lanterns

A glowing idea.

Materials Needed:

Vellum paper, 48 lb., clear

Cutting mat, metal ruler, and X-ACTO knife

Double-sided tape

Spoon

Glass candle holders and votive candles

Instructions:

1. Print out the lanterns on the vellum. Print as many as you like. For best results, manually feed one sheet of vellum at a time. Let dry.
2. For easier folding, score the lantern.
3. Trim the white areas away from all the lantern pages.
4. With the printed side facing down, fold carefully along the scored edges. Using the back of a spoon, press the fold firmly to crease.
5. Attach double-sided tape to the small fold on one side of the lantern. Press firmly to the other side of the lantern, creating a rectangular tube.
6. Light your votive candle and place the lantern around the candle.
7. Enjoy the glow!

Caution: Be sure to use votive candles in glass containers. Never leave the lanterns unattended. Keep out of the reach of children.

Halloween Decorations

Calling all witches, goblins, ghosts and demons. These Halloween projects are guaranteed to raise your spirits. Throw a party and transform your home into a spooky haunted house!

Project 1: Spooky Music CD Labels

BOO! Spooky labels for your spooky sounds.

Materials Needed:

HP CD Label stock

Instructions:

Choose design. Print pdf file onto CD label stock. Let dry.

Project 2: Candy Bag Iron-Ons

Something for the sweet bag.

Happy Halloween

Materials Needed:

HP Iron-On Transfer material

Scissors

Cotton pillowcase or tote bag

Instructions:

1. Print art pages onto iron-on material.

2. Trim around art, leaving 1/4" white space.

3. Follow instructions on transfer material box for ironing on your transfer.

Project 3: Costume Iron-Ons

A fun, fast costume for the little ones.

Materials Needed:

HP Iron-On Transfer material

Scissors

Cotton T-shirt

Instructions:

1. Print art from pdf files onto transfer material. Let dry.

2. Trim all the way around design, leaving 1/4" white space.

3. Follow iron-on transfer directions and iron design onto T-shirt or other material.

Project 4: Stickers

Stick some Halloween flavor anywhere.

Materials Needed:

Full Sheet Label stock

Scissors

Instructions:

1. Print pdf file onto label stock. Let dry.
2. Trim out and apply where desired.

Project 5: Window Clings

Spooky from the outside…

Materials Needed:

Window decal material

Scissors

Instructions:

1. Print pdf file. Let dry.

2. Adhere to window.

Warning: Be sure to use materials designed specifically for your printer. To prevent damage, use window decals specifically designed for laser printers or printers that use heat to fuse the ink.

New Year's Decorations

Uncork the New Year right with lots of fun and easy printable projects!

Project 1: Editable Bottle Label

Cheers!

Materials Needed:

Full Sheet Label stock

Scissors or X-ACTO knife

Instructions:

1. If the pdf contains *Click Here to Edit* or similar instructions, edit the file on screen before printing, otherwise, go to step 2.
2. Print pdf file. Trim white areas away from art.
3. Apply to bottle and give to friends.

Project 4: Masks
Masterfully mysterious!

Materials Needed:

HP Card or Cover stock

Scissors or X-ACTO knife

Ribbon, elastic cord, or wooden dowel

Hole punch

Instructions:

1. Choose design and print pdf file. Let dry.
2. Trim around outside of mask (including eyeholes).
3. Cut small holes on sides with hole punch.
4. Attach a string or elastic cord to side holes. Or, attach a wooden dowel to one side.

CHAPTER **4** CARDS & STATIONERY / Entertaining

Project 5: Coasters

No party fouls in your house!

Materials Needed:

HP Bright White Inkjet paper

Scissors

Cardboard

Self-laminating sheets

Instructions:

1. Print on inkjet paper. Let dry.

2. Glue to cardboard and trim.

3. Laminate coasters to protect ink from spills and condensation.

Correspondence

Everything's nicer when you use the write stuff!

Stationery

With our colorful stationery and notes, you'll have lots to choose from to keep your pen pal interested.

Project 1: Fishing Stationery

Cast your every thought onto paper.

Materials Needed:

HP Bright White Inkjet paper

Instructions:

Print as many copies of the pdf file as desired. Let dry.

Project 2: Fishing Notes

Jot one on the fly.

Materials Needed:

HP Bright White Inkjet paper

Cutting mat, metal ruler, and X-ACTO knife

Instructions:

1. Print as many copies of the pdf file as you want. Let dry.
2. Art is set up 2 per sheet. Trim each page in half so the final size is 5-1/2" x 8-1/2".

Project 3: Golf Stationery
A birdie told me to drop you a line.

Materials Needed:

HP Bright White Inkjet paper

Instructions:

1. Print pdf file. Let dry.

2. Tell 'em about your last score.

Project 4: Golf Notes

Jot it down beFORE you forget it.

Materials Needed:

HP Bright White Inkjet paper

Cutting mat, metal ruler, and X-ACTO knife

Instructions:

1. Print as many copies of the pdf file as you want. Let dry.

2. Art is set up 2 per sheet. Trim each page in half so the final size is 5-1/2" x 8-1/2".

Project 5: Nature Stationery

Bug someone with a letter on this.

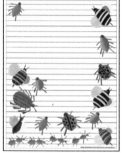

Materials Needed:

HP Bright White Inkjet paper

Instructions:

1. Choose design and print pdf file. Let dry.

2. Write away.

Greeting Cards

Whether you want to say "thanks," "I miss you," "get well," or "happy birthday," these beautifully designed cards are the perfect way to send your thoughts.

Project 1: Birthday Cards

Print one for a friend or family member.

Materials Needed:

HP Greeting Card paper, 1/4-fold or 1/2-fold (ivory or white, matte or glossy)

See Greeting Card Instructions on page 139

Note: Not all birthday cards shown. See CD for additional designs.

Project 2: All-Occasion Cards

They're blank inside, awaiting your message.

Materials Needed:

HP Greeting Card paper, 1/4-fold or 1/2-fold (ivory or white, matte or glossy)

See Greeting Card Instructions on page 139

Note: Not all cards shown. See CD for additional designs.

The following instructions are for HP color inkjet printers, which load from the front. If your printer loads from the back, please consult your printer's user guide. Try printing a test page before using the HP Greeting Card paper.

Greeting Card Instructions:

half-page card

1. Place a sheet of 1/2-fold HP Greeting Card paper (glossy or matte) in your printer tray, glossy/matte side down.
2. Set your printer to *Best* quality.
3. Print page, let dry, and fold in half. (If cropping occurs, select *Shrink to Fit* and reprint.)

quarter-page card

1. Place a sheet of 1/4-fold HP Greeting Card paper (glossy or matte) in your printer tray, glossy/matte side down.
2. Set your printer to *Best* quality.
3. Print page, let dry, and fold in quarters. (If cropping occurs, select *Shrink to Fit* and reprint.)

postcards or 1-panel cards

1. Place a sheet of HP Greeting Card paper (glossy or matte) in your printer tray.
2. Set your printer to *Best* quality.
3. Print the page. (If cropping occurs, select *Shrink to Fit* and reprint.)
4. Cut out card sections.

Chapter 5

HOLIDAYS & EVENTS

Need a reason to celebrate?
Make one of these delightful projects
and you'll be jumping for joy!

Holidays & Events

Winter

Wrap up your winter wonderland!

Christmas

Choose from a wide variety of holiday cards to send to friends and family.

Project 1: Christmas Cards

Spread some good cheer!

Materials Needed:

HP Greeting Card paper (1/2-fold or 1/4-fold)

See Greeting Card Instructions on page 139

Note: Not all Christmas cards shown. See CD for additional designs.

Hanukkah

Spice up your holiday mailings with customizable labels and cards made from the heart. They'll make every package and envelope sparkle with holiday cheer!

Project 1: Hanukkah Cards

Bring smiles to your friends and loved ones.

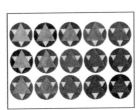

Materials Needed:

HP Greeting Card paper (1/2-fold or 1/4-fold)

See Greeting Card Instructions on page 139

Project 2: Hanukkah Address Labels

To you.

Materials Needed:

Avery White Address Labels (#8162)

Instructions:

1. Customize your address labels before printing or delete to make blank.
2. Print pdf file. Let dry.
3. Use them for all your mailings.

Project 3: Hanukkah Return Labels

From me.

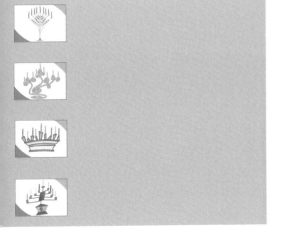

Materials Needed:

Avery White Return Address Labels (#8167)

Instructions:

1. Customize your labels before printing. You only need to type it in once, and the rest of the fields will automatically duplicate.
2. Print pdf file. Let dry.
3. Use them for all your mailings.

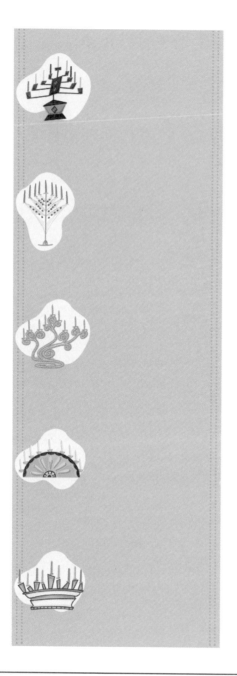

Project 4: Hanukkah Shipping Labels

Special delivery with sparkle!

Materials Needed:

Avery White Shipping Labels (#8463)

Instructions:

1. Customize your shipping labels before printing, or delete to make blank.
2. Print pdf file on label paper. Let dry.
3. Use them for all your mailings.

Hint: Try using these as customized gift tags.

Kwanzaa

So festive! Bring vibrant colors to all of your gifts with these cute boxes.

Project 1: Gift Boxes

Make them cheer with joy.

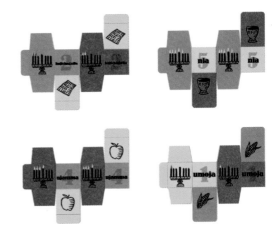

Materials Needed:

HP Card or Cover stock

Cutting mat, metal ruler, and X-ACTO knife

Glue or double-sided tape

Instructions:

1. Print pdf file on card stock. Let dry.
2. Cut out box around outside edges.
3. Fold along lines where indicated.
4. Apply glue or double-sided tape where indicated.

Tip: To make folding easier, score along lines with butter knife or scoring tool first. Not all boxes shown. See CD for additional designs.

New Year's Supper Club Kit

If you're planning to host a dinner party, you can turn it into a truly festive affair. Here are some matching favors that will help you create a gathering to remember. Whether it's wine and cheese or a full buffet, your efforts will surely have them coming back for seconds.

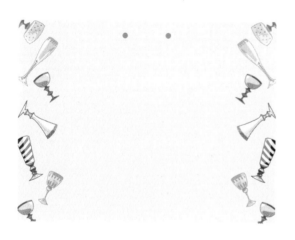

Project 1: Editable Invitation

This will get everyone in the mood.

Materials Needed:

1 or more sheets HP Card or Cover stock

1 or more sheets vellum paper, 48 lb., clear

Cutting mat, metal ruler, and X-ACTO knife

1/8" hole punch and scissors

Ribbon 1/4" wide (4" lengths)

A-7 envelopes (5-1/4" x 7-1/4")

Instructions:

1. Customize page 1 of the pdf (it will repeat automatically). Print on vellum and let dry. Print as many as you need (2 to a page).
2. Print page 2 onto card stock. Print the same number of sheets as page 1.
3. Trim white areas away from vellum.
4. Trim white areas away from card stock.
5. With the vellum and card stock face-up, center the vellum over the card stock piece.
6. Holding the two together, punch out the two gray dots at the top.
7. Cut the ribbon into 4" lengths (one for each invitation).
8. Thread ribbon through holes or tie a bow in front to hold the two pieces together.

Project 2: Editable Place Cards

Guests will feel special when they see their names on these cards.

Materials Needed:

1 or more sheets HP Card or Cover stock

Cutting mat, metal ruler, and X-ACTO knife

Scoring tool or butter knife

Spoon

Instructions:

1. Customize the cards before printing, or delete the fields to make them blank.
2. Print as many cards as you need. There are 4 cards per sheet. Let dry.
3. For easier folding, score the place cards. To do this, lay a ruler along each set of dotted lines and run a scoring tool along the ruler. Use medium pressure to make an indentation in the paper.
4. Trim away all white areas.
5. With each card face down, fold along the scored edge. Crease with the back of a spoon.
6. Stand the place cards at each person's plate.

Project 3: Editable Menu Cards

Your carefully planned dinner will have a place of honor here.

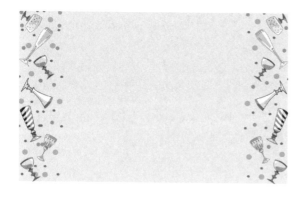

Materials Needed:

1 or more sheets of HP Card or Cover stock

Cutting mat, metal ruler, and X-ACTO knife

Instructions:

1. Customize the menu card by typing your dinner menu in the first card. It will repeat itself automatically in the second card.
2. Print the menu cards on card stock. Print as many as you need (there are 2 cards per page). Let dry.
3. Trim away white areas from each page.
4. Place a menu card at each table setting.

Project 4: Glass Charms

Always know which drink is yours with these gorgeous, customizable glass charms.

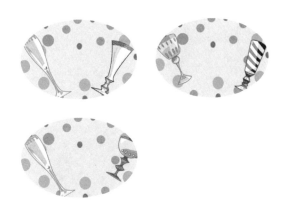

Materials Needed:

1 or more sheets vellum paper, 48 lb., clear

Scissors

Hole punch

Ribbon 1/4" wide (5" lengths)

Instructions:

1. Customize the charms before printing.
2. Print as many charms as you need on the vellum paper. There are 28 charms per sheet. For best results, manually feed one piece of vellum at a time. Let dry.
3. Using scissors, cut out each glass charm.
4. Punch a hole in the gray dot on each charm.
5. Cut 5" lengths of ribbon for each. Slip one end through the hole and attach each charm by tying a bow around the stem of the glass.

Project 5: Lanterns

Light up the night like never before.

Materials Needed:

1 or more sheets of vellum paper, 48 lb., clear

Cutting mat, metal ruler, and X-ACTO knife

Double-sided tape

Spoon

Glass candle holders and votive candles

Instructions:

1. Print pdf file on the vellum. Print as many as you like. Print all three sizes or any combination. For best results, manually feed one sheet at a time. Let dry.
2. Score the lantern where indicated.
3. Trim away white areas from all pages.
4. With the printed side facing down, fold carefully along the scored edges. Crease with the back of a spoon.
5. Attach double-sided tape to the small fold on one side of the lantern. Press firmly to the other side, creating a rectangular tube.
6. Light your votive candles and place the lantern around the candle.
7. Enjoy the glow!

Caution: Be sure to use votive candles in glass containers. Never leave the lanterns unattended. Keep them out of the reach of children.

Project 6: Napkin Rings

Fold your elegant napkins in style.

Materials Needed:

1 or more sheets of vellum paper, 48 lb., clear

Cutting mat, metal ruler, and X-ACTO knife

Double-sided tape

Instructions:

1. Print as many napkin rings as you need on the vellum. Manually feed one sheet of vellum at a time. Let dry completely.
2. Trim away all white areas.
3. Wrap the napkin ring around a napkin.
4. Use the double-sided tape to attach both ends of the napkin ring together.
5. Set an elegant table for your guests.

Valentine Wrap Sets

Be still my heart!

Time to share the love.

Project 1: Wrapping Paper

Special paper for small, special packages.

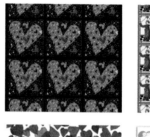 

Materials Needed:

HP Bright White Inkjet paper

Instructions:

1. Print as many pages of wrapping paper as you like. Let dry completely.
2. Wrap up something special.

Tip: You can also use the wrapping paper for fun background paper in a scrapbook or journal.

Project 2: Gift Bags

Something for your sweetie.

Materials Needed:

HP Card or Cover stock

Cutting mat, metal ruler, and X-ACTO knife

Double-sided tape

Scoring tool and spoon

Instructions:

1. Print two copies of pdf file. Let dry.
2. Trim around the outside edges.
3. Score and fold along all solid lines.
4. Glue the two sides together where indicated.
5. Fold in the white flap at bottom.
6. Fold in large flaps, gluing the back of the last one to seal the bottom of the bag.

Project 3: Gift Tags

With hugs and kisses.

Materials Needed:

HP Card or Cover stock

Cutting mat, metal ruler, and X-ACTO knife

Scoring tool

Instructions:

1. Print pdf file on card stock. There are 2 cards to a page. Let dry.
2. Score where indicated.
3. Trim around outside of cards.
4. Fold in half and write your message.
5. Slip on top of a package or in a gift bag.

Project 4: Gift Boxes

Good things come in small packages.

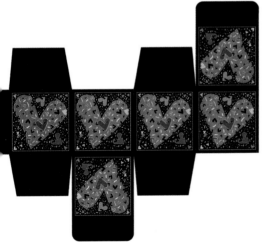

Materials Needed:

HP Card or Cover stock

Cutting mat, metal ruler, and X-ACTO knife

Scoring tool

Double-sided tape or glue

Instructions:

1. Print pdf file on card stock. Let dry.
2. Trim around outside edges.
3. Score and fold along lines where indicated.
4. Apply glue or double-sided tape where indicated.

Spring

Colorful celebration goodies galore!

St. Patrick's Day Tableware

It's our lucky day! Now you can share the magic with all of your visiting leprechauns.

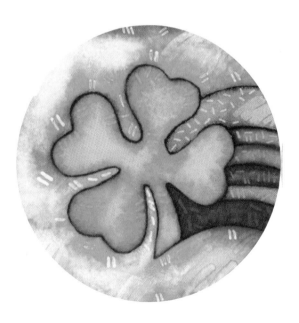

Project 1: Coasters

For your lucky lager.

Materials Needed:

HP Bright White Inkjet paper

Scissors

Self-laminating sheets

Instructions:

1. Print on inkjet paper. Let dry.
2. Cover with self-laminating sheets to protect ink from spills.
3. Glue paper to cardboard.
4. Cut out each coaster.

Note: Not all coasters shown. See CD for additional designs.

Project 2: Cup Wrappers
Make 'em festive.

Materials Needed:

HP Bright White Inkjet paper

Scissors

Tape

Instructions:

1. If the pdf contains *Click Here to Edit* or similar instructions, edit the file on screen before printing, otherwise, go to step 2.

2. Cut out artwork.

3. Tape ends together to form a circle.

Easter Decorations

The traditional egg hunt. The chance to wear your new bonnet. There is nothing like Easter. Here are some projects to boost up the fun level.

Project 1: Easter Stickers

A decorating shortcut to beautiful Easter eggs.

Materials Needed:

Full Sheet Label stock

Scissors

Instructions:

1. Print pdf file onto label stock. Let dry.
2. Cut out desired design and place on eggs or Easter baskets—anywhere you want a little color.

Note: Not all sticker designs shown. See CD for additional pdf files.

Project 2: Egg Dress-Up Kit

Your eggs can be works of art too.

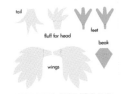

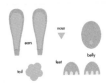

Materials Needed:

5 or more dyed eggs

2 or more sheets of card stock

Cutting mat, metal ruler, and X-ACTO knife

Butter knife or scoring tool

Pencil

Small hot-glue gun

Embellishments such as google-eyes, yarn

Tweezers (to hold small objects while gluing)

Instructions:

1. Print the egg decorations and stands onto card stock. Set aside to dry completely.

2. For easier folding, score all the tabs.

3. Trim the white areas away from all the decorations and stands.

4. Apply a small bead of glue to one end of an egg stand and connect the ends to form a ring.

5. Apply a dot of glue to your egg and then quickly add your decoration.

Note: Not all designs shown. See CD for additional pdf files.

Project 3: Spring Pinwheels

Spring into breezy weather with these colorful pinwheels.

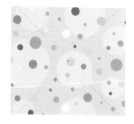

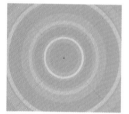

Materials Needed:

HP Premium Inkjet paper

Cutting mat, metal ruler, and X-ACTO knife

White craft glue

Wooden dowels

Push pins and straight pins

Spray adhesive and newspaper

Instructions:

1. Print pdf files. Let dry.
2. Cut out the squares.
3. Place squares face down on newspaper. Spray the backs with adhesive and let dry.
4. Place one square on top of the other. Line up edges and press firmly into place.
5. Cut along dotted lines to make spokes.
6. See CD for instructions to attach to dowel.

Earth Day

Every day is Earth Day!

In all things of nature there is something of the marvelous.

Aristotle

Project 1: Iron-Ons

Plant a tree and design a T-shirt!

Materials Needed:

HP Iron-On Transfer paper

Scissors

Iron and cotton T-shirt

Instructions:

1. Print pdf file onto transfer paper. Let dry.
2. Trim around design, leaving 1/4" white space.
3. Follow iron-on transfer box instructions for adhering to T-shirt.

Warning: Do not use iron-on transfer material with any laser printer or printer that uses heat to fuse the ink. It may melt the material and damage the printer.

Cinco De Mayo

Celebrate this special day in style with our festive decorations.

Project 1: 3D Flowers

Accent walls, windows, and senoritas' hair!

Materials Needed:

HP Bright White Inkjet paper

Scissors

Glue or double-sided tape

Instructions:

1. Print one sheet for each flower you wish to make. Let dry.
2. Cut out all petals, leaves, and center.
3. Glue or tape petal to itself where indicated.
4. Arrange four petals on a table or other flat surface, and then tape the petals together at the points in the center.
5. Repeat step 4 for the other four petals.
6. Put the second group of four petals on top of the first group and attach.
7. Attach the center to the assembled flower petals.
8. Attach the leaves to the outside of the assembled flowers. Be artistic!

Project 2: Flags

For the fiesta.

Materials Needed:

HP Premium Inkjet paper

Self-laminating sheets

Instructions:

1. Print as many copies of the pdf files as you like. Let dry.
2. Laminate flags to protect ink before using outside.
3. Decorate and use as is, or paste them back to back and attach wooden dowels to the side to make mini flagpoles.

Mother's Day Gift Set

The colorful flowers adorning these items are sure to put a smile on Mom's face.

Project 1: Editable Card

So perfect.

Materials Needed:

HP Greeting Card paper, 1/2-fold

Instructions:

1. If the pdf contains *Click Here to Edit* or similar instructions, edit the file on screen before printing, otherwise, go to step 2.
2. Set your print quality to *Best*.
3. Print a test of page 1. If cropping occurs, select *Shrink to Fit*, and print again to ensure sizing.
4. Print page 1 onto greeting card paper, and leave it in the printer tray to dry completely.
5. Remove the printed page from the printer tray and, without turning the page over, return it to the loading tray.
6. Print page 2 and finish with a fold.

Project 2: Magnets

Attractive statements for Mom.

Materials Needed:

Printable Magnetic Inkjet paper

Cutting mat, metal ruler, and X-ACTO knife

Instructions:

1. Print the artwork onto the magnetic sheets.
   Let dry.
2. Cut out each magnet as indicated.

Project 3: Photo Frame
Say cheese!

Materials Needed:

1 or more sheets of HP Card stock or Printable Magnetic paper

Cutting mat, metal ruler, and X-ACTO knife

Instructions:

1. Print the frame onto card stock or magnetic paper. Let dry.

2. Trim the white areas away from the frame, including the picture window.

3. If your frame is printed on card stock, tape your photo in place from the back.

4. If you printed the frame on magnetic paper, put your photo behind the frame and attach it to any suitable metal surface.

Project 4: Gift Tags

A snazzy topping to a gift.

Materials Needed:

HP Card or Cover stock

Cutting mat, metal ruler, and X-ACTO knife

Instructions:

1. Choose design and print pdf file. Let dry.

2. Trim where indicated.

3. Write your message and attach to gift.

Hint: You can either fold these cards in half or leave them flat. Punch a hole in the card and tie to your package with ribbon or raffia.

Project 5: World's Best Mom T-Shirt Iron-On

Show the world she's the best.

Materials Needed:

HP Inkjet Iron-On Transfer material

Scissors

Iron and cotton T-shirt

Instructions:

1. Print pdf file onto transfer paper. Let dry.
2. Trim around design, leaving 1/4" white space.
3. Follow iron-on transfer box instructions for adhering to T-shirt.

Warning: Do not use iron-on transfer material with any laser printer or printer that uses heat to fuse the ink. It may melt the material and damage the printer.

Graduation

All the exciting parties and events at graduation can be remembered with this lovely keepsake.

Project 1: Gatherings Book

Gather friends…gather memories.

Gatherings
Celebrating memories with family and friends

Materials Needed:

11 sheets of card stock

1 sheet of vellum paper, 48 lb., clear

Double-sided tape

Cutting mat, metal ruler, and X-ACTO knife

Butter knife or scoring tool

Spoon

Ribbon, 1" wide, 1-1/2 yards

Scissors

Photos

See Instructions on page 176

Gatherings Book

(continued)

*Cover and Spine PDF
Instructions:*

1. Print the book cover (pgs. 1–3 of pdf) onto card stock. Print page 3 twice. Let dry.

2. Trim the white areas away from covers.

3. Print the accordion spine (pg. 4 of pdf) onto the card stock. Let dry.

4. For easier folding, score the accordion spine. There are 9 lines to score.

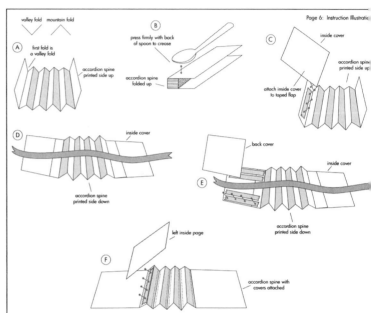

5. With the accordion spine printed side up, fold up the first tab that is marked *tape inside cover*. Continue folding the scored lines back and forth. See illustration A.

6. Using the back of a spoon, press the folds firmly to crease. See illustration B.

7. Unfold the spine with printed side up. Place double-sided tape along the left tab marked *tape inside cover*. Attach one of the inside covers on the tape, carefully aligning the edge of the cover with the crease in the spine. Press firmly in place. See illustration C.

8. Repeat step 7 with the right tab and inside cover.

9. Flip the spine over, printed side down, and center the ribbon across the inside covers and spine. See illustration D.

10. Apply double-sided tape to the back of the inside cover on the left, leaving the area around the ribbon free from tape. See illustration E.

11. Place the back cover on top, aligning the purple band with the edge of the spine. Make sure the ribbon does not get stuck to the tape.

Gatherings Book

Instructions (continued):

12. Repeat steps 10 and 11 to attach the front cover.

Inside Pages PDF Instructions:

1. Print the inside pages (pgs. 1–6) onto card stock. Print pages 3 and 4 twice. Let dry.

2. Trim the white areas away from the inside pages. Keep the pages stacked in this order: 3, 1, 2, 5, 6, 4.

3. Place the spine, with covers attached, face up. Place double-sided tape on the left side of the first accordion peak where indicated. Attach the first left page from the stack, aligning the edge of the inside page with the white dotted line along the accordion peak. See illustration F.

4. Repeat step 3 for the next page by placing tape along the right side of the accordion peak. In addition, apply tape to the back of the left inside page to secure the pages together.

5. Attach the first right page from the stack, aligning the edge of the inside page with the white dotted line along the accordion peak. Press pages together firmly.

6. Continue attaching the rest of the inside pages by repeating steps 3 and 4.

7. Once complete, place your book out for family and friends to share their thoughts and memories.

Photo Corners Instructions:

1. Print the photo corners (pg. 5 of the cover pdf) onto the vellum paper. Let dry.

2. Trim the white areas away from art.

3. Make a slit along the dark line in each.

4. Slip one photo corner onto each corner of your picture.

5. Apply double-sided tape to the photo corners on the picture. Carefully place the picture and press the corners firmly.

Note: Instructions and full-size illustrated instruction diagram are on the CD.

Project 3: Greatest Dad Photo Frame

Just the two of you…

Materials Needed:

Printable Magnetic Inkjet paper or HP Card or Cover stock

Cutting mat, metal ruler, and X-ACTO knife

Photo

Instructions:

1. Print the frame onto magnetic paper or card stock. Let dry.
2. Trim the white areas away from the frame, including the picture window.
3. If your frame is printed on magnetic paper, put your photo behind the frame and attach it to any suitable metal surface.
4. If your frame is printed on card stock, tape your photo in place from the back.

Project 4: Magnets

Remind him everyday!

Materials Needed:

Printable Magnetic Inkjet paper

Cutting mat, metal ruler, and X-ACTO knife

Instructions:

1. Print the artwork onto the magnetic sheets. Let dry.
2. Cut out each magnet as indicated.

Summer

Sunshine, lollipops, and rainbows everywhere!

Lemonade Stand Kit

Hot off the press! Ice cold lemonade signs and banners!

Project 1: Signs

For the junior entrepreneur.

Materials Needed:

HP Bright White Inkjet paper

Instructions:

1. Print pdf files.
2. Hang them around the neighborhood and sell, sell, sell.

Project 2: Banner

This banner makes a statement.

Materials Needed:

HP Banner paper

HP Bright White Inkjet paper (optional)

Instructions:

1. Follow printer set-up instructions on the back of the HP Banner paper box.
2. Insert a four-sheet length of banner paper into the printer, with the top cut edge pointing toward the printer.
3. Open the banner pdf file on your screen. In the File menu, select *Print Setup*.
4. In Print Setup, select the *Properties* button.
5. In Properties, select the section on *Paper*.
6. In Paper, make sure *Banner* is selected under Paper Type. Click OK.
7. Click OK again to close the other window.
8. Print pages 2 to 5 of pdf file.

Option: If not using banner paper, print pages 2 to 5 of pdf on regular paper and tape pages together. You may need to trim edges and overlap the pages slightly to prevent gaps from showing.

Project 3: Luminaria

Perfect for illuminating outdoor fun until the twilights last gleaming.

Materials Needed:

Lunch bags (brown or white)

Scissors

Glass candle holders and votive candles

Instructions:

1. Place a standard lunch bag (bottom flap down) on a piece of 8-1/2" x 11" paper.
2. Tape the top (open) edge of the brown bag to the top edge of the paper.
3. To print, manually feed the bag and paper into the printer with the bag side facing down. Set aside to dry completely.
4. Trim along top edge of artwork to create an interesting shape.
5. Put some sand inside the bag for weight.
6. Place a small candle in a glass holder inside the bag. Enjoy!

Caution: Be sure to use votive candles in glass containers. Never leave the luminaria bags unattended. Keep out of the reach of children.

Project 4: Table Tents

Great way to label Aunt Margo's potato salad at your next family reunion or potluck.

Materials Needed:

1 or more sheets of card stock

Cutting mat, metal ruler, and X-ACTO knife

Scoring tool or butter knife

Spoon

Instructions:

1. Customize the table tents before printing. Type your guests' names or menu items.
2. Print as many table tents on the card stock as you need. There are 4 to a sheet. Let dry.
3. For easier folding, score the table tents. To do this, lay a ruler along each set of dotted lines and, with medium pressure, run a butter knife or scoring tool along the ruler.
4. Trim the white areas away from all pages.
5. With each place card face down, fold carefully along the scored edge. Using the back of a spoon, press the fold firmly to crease.

Project 5: String Lights

String them anywhere you want the soft glow of stars and stripes.

Materials Needed:

8 or more sheets of vellum paper, 48 lb., clear
Cutting mat, metal ruler, and X-ACTO knife
Tape
Butter knife or scoring tool
String of Christmas lights (white or green)

Instructions:

1. Print the art on vellum. Manually feed one piece at a time. There are 2 light covers per page. Let dry.
2. Score the covers where indicated.
3. Cut out the two light holes on each cover.
4. Cut along the slit where indicated.
5. Cut around outside edge of each light cover.
6. With art facing down, fold along scored lines.
7. Holding the light bulb facing the ground, take the short tab and slip over the bulb.
8. Fold the square in half, bringing the long tab over the wire towards you. Insert this tab into the slit. The entire length of the tab should be in the slit. Then fit the light hole from the long tab over the bulb on the interior of the light cover.
9. Bend and tape the top part of the long tab to the inside of the light cover. Secure in place with tape.
10. Plug in your lights.

Summer Grilling

The lazy days are upon us, which means it's time for that traditional rite of summer—barbecue. Kick off the grilling season in style!

Project 1: Apron Iron-On

Grill chefs will love this smokin' apron design.

Materials Needed:

HP Inkjet Iron-On Transfer material

Scissors

Cotton apron

Iron

Instructions:

1. Print pdf file onto transfer paper. Let dry.
2. Trim around design, leaving 1/4" white space.
3. Follow iron-on transfer box instructions for adhering to apron front.

Warning: Do not use iron-on transfer material with any laser printer or printer that uses heat to fuse the ink. It may melt the material and damage the printer.

Project 2: Customizable Sauce Label

Whatever the ingredients, our red-hot label design will add zest to your special blend.

Materials Needed:

Full Sheet White Sticker paper

Cutting mat, metal ruler, and X-ACTO knife

Glass jar

Instructions:

1. Customize the labels by adding your name, sauce type, and date where indicated in the pdf file.
2. Print art onto sticker paper and let dry.
3. Cut out along the label edge.
4. Apply to the jar and give to friends and family.

Hint: To remove a label from a jar, simply soak in warm, soapy water.

Project 3: Recipe Cards

Customizable or with blank lines. Hot, hot, hot!

Materials Needed:

HP Card or Cover stock

Cutting mat, metal ruler, and X-ACTO knife

Self-laminating sheets (optional)

Instructions:

1. If the pdf contains *Click Here to Edit* or similar instructions, edit the file on screen before printing, otherwise, go to step 2.
2. Trim recipe cards where indicated.
3. Share your secrets with friends and family.

Hint: Store recipe cards in plastic sleeves or cover them with self-laminating sheets to protect from kitchen spills.

Fall

Back to school, and back to the kitchen!

Tabletop Football

Play the classic tabletop football game using these printable football and goalpost projects.

Project 1: Football and Goalpost

Time for kick off!

Materials Needed:

HP Bright White Inkjet paper

Tape or glue

Cutting mat, metal ruler, and X-ACTO knife

Instructions:

1. Print one copy of football page. Let dry.
2. Cut out design along the outside black lines.
3. Fold in a triangular pattern five times (use the two black lines at the bottom as a starting point).
4. On the sixth fold, make a smaller triangular fold.
5. On the seventh fold, tuck the flap into the "pocket."
6. The "laces" should appear on either side.
7. Print two copies of goalpost page. Let dry.
8. Cut out both goalposts along outside edge.
9. Fold all of the white tabs back.
10. Fold along the black lines (on green rectangles) to form base.
11. Fold green base up and attach to pole.
12. Align the goalposts back to back and glue or tape matching tabs together.

Project 1: How to Play
(continued)

How to Play:

1. Find a flat, square-edge tabletop about two feet wide (like the school cafeteria kind), and have the players sit across the table from each other.

2. To kick off, use one finger to prop the paper football up on one point. Position the ball on the table near the edge you're kicking from. Use a strong finger-flick to "kick" the ball, trying to get it to land as far across the table as you can. If the ball goes over the opposite edge, it's a touchback and the other player gets the ball at his or her "20-yard line."

3. At the kickoff, if the ball lands hanging over the edge (in touchdown position) of the opposite side of the table, it's a safety. The kicker gets two points. The other player now has to kick off.

4. The player in control of the ball gets two flicks (also called downs) to try to score a touchdown. A touchdown is scored when you get the ball to hang over the other side of the table without falling off. Each time you flick the football, it's a "down."

5. If the ball falls off the edge of the table during a down, the opposing player gets the ball at his or her 20-yard line.

6. After a touchdown, have the opposing player try to flick the ball through the goalpost.

7. After a touchdown, a player can choose to "go for two" instead of kicking a field goal. In this case, the ball is placed on the 20-yard line near the other player's side of the table. If the player gets the ball to hang over the edge in a touchdown position in one flick, he or she gets two points.

Back to School

Help keep your student organized and in style with these binder covers that are both cool and functional.

Project 1: Binder Covers

Too cool for school!

Materials Needed:

HP Bright White Inkjet paper

3-ring binder with clear cover

Instructions:

1. If the pdf contains *Click Here to Edit* or similar instructions, edit the file on screen before printing, otherwise, go to step 2.
2. Print pdf file. Let dry.
3. Slide art under clear binder cover.

Halloween

Have you seen the costs of Halloween masks lately? Now, that's scary! Especially when you can make your own booootiful ones from home.

Project 1: Halloween Masks

Surprise someone with a new face.

Materials Needed:

HP Card or Cover stock

Scissors and hole punch

Elastic cord or string

Self-laminating sheets (optional)

Instructions:

1. Print pdf file. Let dry. Laminate page to protect ink from the elements.

2. Cut out masks and eyeholes.

3. Cut out small side holes with hole punch.

4. Attach string or elastic cord to side holes.

Note: Not all designs shown. See CD for all pdf files.

Thanksgiving Kids' Table

Give the kids a special table of their own with all kinds of fun and entertaining decorations.

Project 1: Placemat Puzzles

Entertainment at the table.

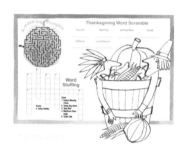

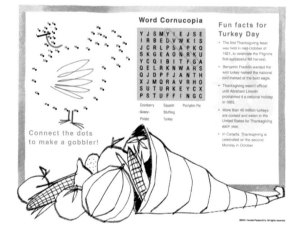

Materials Needed:

HP Bright White Inkjet paper

Pens or pencils

Instructions:

1. Print pdf files. Let dry.
2. Put on the table with pens and pencils for the kids to solve while they wait for dinner or dessert.

Project 2: Placemats

Have some fun with dinner.

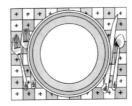 

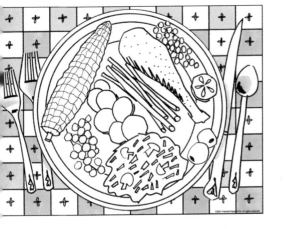

Materials Needed:

HP Bright White Inkjet paper

Scissors

Coloring crayons

Double-sided tape

Instructions:

1. Print the coloring placemat pdf. Let dry.

2. Print pages 1 to 2 of the the food cutout pdf file. Let dry.

3. Put on the table with crayons and double-sided tape. Let the kids be creative and have fun.

Project 3: Table Decorations

Give thanks and have a little fun.

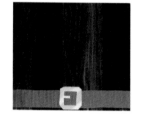

Materials Needed:

HP Brochure and Flyer paper

Scissors

Double-sided tape

Instructions:

1. Print headband pdf pages. Let dry.
2. Trim along dotted lines.
3. Attach back of headband to headpiece with tape at each end.

Note: Refer to specific instructions on the CD for turkey or pilgrim hat table decoration.

Project 4: Place Cards

Mix it up a bit!

Materials Needed:

HP Brochure and Flyer paper

Cutting mat, metal ruler, and X-ACTO knife

Instructions:

1. Edit the place cards before printing, or delete field to leave blank. Let dry.
2. Trim cards where indicated.
3. Fold in half
4. Put at each place setting.

Project 5: Coasters

To catch those pesky drips.

Materials Needed:

HP Card or Cover stock

Scissors

Self-laminating sheets

Instructions:

1. Print pdf file. Let dry.

2. Cover with laminating sheets.

3. Cut out each coaster.

Project 6: Window Cling
Gobble. Gobble. Gobble.

Materials Needed:

Window decals for inkjet printers

Scissors

Instructions:

1. Print pdf file. Let dry.
2. Trim instructions off top and adhere to window.

Warning: Be sure to use materials designed specifically for your printer. To prevent damage, use window decals specifically designed for laser printers or printers that use heat to fuse the ink.

creating your own great dvds & cds

upgrading your hp pavilion pc

hp pavilion pcs made easy

mark l. chambers

© 2003, paper, 368 pages,
0-13-100105-1

Make the most of any DVD or
CD recorder with this book.
Through start-to-finish projects,
you'll learn to create every type
of DVD, CD, and VCD, and record
whatever you want — video,
photographs, music, or data.
Coverage includes choosing the
right recorder, installation, formats,
software tools, slide shows, labels,
on-disc menus, troubleshooting —
even the latest DVD writers!

tom sheldon

© 2003, paper, 736 pages,
0-13-100415-8

Make your desktop HP Pavilion
PC better, faster, and more useful!
Whatever HP Pavilion you own —
old or new — this HP authorized
guide shows you exactly how to
supercharge it! One step at a time,
long-time PC expert Tom Sheldon
shows you what to buy, what to
do, and exactly how to do it. It's
cheaper than you think — and
easier than you ever imagined!

nancy stevenson

© 2003, paper, 416 pages,
0-13-100251-1

Make the most of your new desktop
HP Pavilion PC and Windows XP!
This book covers all you need to
get productive with your desktop
Pavilion fast — and have more fun,
too! This book is a complete, easy
introduction to your Pavilion computer and Microsoft®'s Windows®
XP. Easily master XP's amazing
collection of tools and learn to
configure XP exactly the way you
want it. Sure, there are other
introductory PC books — but this
is the only one that's authorized by
HP, and written just for you, the
Pavilion owner!

www.phptr.com

the official hp guides

www.hp.com/hpbooks

free subscription

Want to know about new products, services and solutions from Hewlett-Packard Company — as soon as they're invented?

Need information about new HP services to help you implement new or existing products?

Looking for HP's newest solution to a specific challenge in your business?

inview features the latest from HP!

4 easy ways to subscribe, and it's FREE:

- **fax** complete and fax the form below to (651) 430-3388, or

- **online** sign up online at www.hp.com/go/inview, or

- **email** complete the information below and send to hporders@earthlink.net, or

- **mail** complete and mail the form below to:

Twin Cities Fulfillment Center
Hewlett-Packard Company
P.O. Box 408
Stillwater, MN 55082

invent

reply now and don't miss an issue!

name	title
company	dept./mail stop
address	
city	state	zip

email   signature   date

please indicate your industry below:

- ☐ accounting
- ☐ education
- ☐ financial services
- ☐ government
- ☐ healthcare/medical
- ☐ legal
- ☐ manufacturing
- ☐ publishing/printing
- ☐ online services
- ☐ real estate
- ☐ retail/wholesale distrib
- ☐ technical
- ☐ telecommunications
- ☐ transport and travel
- ☐ utilities
- ☐ other: _____

LICENSE AGREEMENT AND LIMITED WARRANTY

READ THE FOLLOWING TERMS AND CONDITIONS CAREFULLY BEFORE OPENING THIS SOFTWARE MEDIA PACKAGE. THIS LEGAL DOCUMENT IS AN AGREEMENT BETWEEN YOU AND PRENTICE-HALL, INC. (THE "COMPANY"). BY OPENING THIS SEALED SOFTWARE MEDIA PACKAGE, YOU ARE AGREEING TO BE BOUND BY THESE TERMS AND CONDITIONS. IF YOU DO NOT AGREE WITH THESE TERMS AND CONDITIONS, DO NOT OPEN THE SOFTWARE MEDIA PACKAGE. PROMPTLY RETURN THE UNOPENED SOFTWARE MEDIA PACKAGE AND ALL ACCOMPANYING ITEMS TO THE PLACE YOU OBTAINED THEM FOR A FULL REFUND OF ANY SUMS YOU HAVE PAID.

1.   **GRANT OF LICENSE:** In consideration of your payment of the license fee, which is part of the price you paid for this product, and your agreement to abide by the terms and conditions of this Agreement, the Company grants to you a nonexclusive right to use and display the copy of the enclosed software program (hereinafter the "SOFTWARE") on a single computer (i.e., with a single CPU) at a single location so long as you comply with the terms of this Agreement. The Company reserves all rights not expressly granted to you under this Agreement.

2.   **OWNERSHIP OF SOFTWARE:** You own only the magnetic or physical media (the enclosed software media) on which the SOFTWARE is recorded or fixed, but the Company retains all the rights, title, and ownership to the SOFTWARE recorded on the original software media copy(ies) and all subsequent copies of the SOFTWARE, regardless of the form or media on which the original or other copies may exist. This license is not a sale of the original SOFTWARE or any copy to you.

3.   **COPY RESTRICTIONS:** This SOFTWARE and the accompanying printed materials and user manual (the "Documentation") are the subject of copyright. You may not copy the Documentation or the SOFTWARE, except that you may make a single copy of the SOFTWARE for backup or archival purposes only. You may be held legally responsible for any copying or copyright infringement which is caused or encouraged by your failure to abide by the terms of this restriction.

4.   **USE RESTRICTIONS:** You may not network the SOFTWARE or otherwise use it on more than one computer or computer terminal at the same time. You may physically transfer the SOFTWARE from one computer to another provided that the SOFTWARE is used on only one computer at a time. You may not distribute copies of the SOFTWARE or Documentation to others. You may not reverse engineer, disassemble, decompile, modify, adapt, translate, or create derivative works based on the SOFTWARE or the Documentation without the prior written consent of the Company.

5.   **TRANSFER RESTRICTIONS:** The enclosed SOFTWARE is licensed only to you and may not be transferred to any one else without the prior written consent of the Company. Any unauthorized transfer of the SOFTWARE shall result in the immediate termination of this Agreement.

6.   **TERMINATION:** This license is effective until terminated. This license will terminate automatically without notice from the Company and become null and void if you fail to comply with any provisions or limitations of this license. Upon termination, you shall destroy the Documentation and all copies of the SOFTWARE. All provisions of this Agreement as to warranties, limitation of liability, remedies or damages, and our ownership rights shall survive termination.

7.   **MISCELLANEOUS:** This Agreement shall be construed in accordance with the laws of the United States of America and the State of New York and shall benefit the Company, its affiliates, and assignees.

8.   **LIMITED WARRANTY AND DISCLAIMER OF WARRANTY:** The Company warrants that the SOFTWARE, when properly used in accordance with the Documentation, will operate in substantial conformity with the description of the SOFTWARE set forth in the Documentation. The Company does not warrant that the SOFTWARE will meet your requirements or that the operation of the SOFTWARE will be uninterrupted or error-free. The Company warrants that the media on which the SOFTWARE is delivered shall be free from defects in materials and workmanship under normal use for a period of thirty (30) days from the date of your purchase. Your only remedy and the Company's only obligation under these limited warranties is, at the Company's option, return of the warranted item for a refund of any amounts paid by you or replacement of the item. Any replacement of SOFTWARE or media under the warranties shall not extend the original warranty period. The limited warranty set forth above shall not apply to any SOFTWARE which the Company determines in good faith has been subject to misuse, neglect, improper installation, repair, alteration, or damage by you. EXCEPT FOR THE EXPRESSED WARRANTIES SET FORTH ABOVE, THE COMPANY

DISCLAIMS ALL WARRANTIES, EXPRESS OR IMPLIED, INCLUDING WITHOUT LIMITATION, THE IMPLIED WARRANTIES OF MERCHANTABILITY AND FITNESS FOR A PARTICULAR PURPOSE. EXCEPT FOR THE EXPRESS WARRANTY SET FORTH ABOVE, THE COMPANY DOES NOT WARRANT, GUARANTEE, OR MAKE ANY REPRESENTATION REGARDING THE USE OR THE RESULTS OF THE USE OF THE SOFTWARE IN TERMS OF ITS CORRECTNESS, ACCURACY, RELIABILITY, CURRENTNESS, OR OTHERWISE.

IN NO EVENT, SHALL THE COMPANY OR ITS EMPLOYEES, AGENTS, SUPPLIERS, OR CONTRACTORS BE LIABLE FOR ANY INCIDENTAL, INDIRECT, SPECIAL, OR CONSEQUENTIAL DAMAGES ARISING OUT OF OR IN CONNECTION WITH THE LICENSE GRANTED UNDER THIS AGREEMENT, OR FOR LOSS OF USE, LOSS OF DATA, LOSS OF INCOME OR PROFIT, OR OTHER LOSSES, SUSTAINED AS A RESULT OF INJURY TO ANY PERSON, OR LOSS OF OR DAMAGE TO PROPERTY, OR CLAIMS OF THIRD PARTIES, EVEN IF THE COMPANY OR AN AUTHORIZED REPRESENTATIVE OF THE COMPANY HAS BEEN ADVISED OF THE POSSIBILITY OF SUCH DAMAGES. IN NO EVENT SHALL LIABILITY OF THE COMPANY FOR DAMAGES WITH RESPECT TO THE SOFTWARE EXCEED THE AMOUNTS ACTUALLY PAID BY YOU, IF ANY, FOR THE SOFTWARE.

SOME JURISDICTIONS DO NOT ALLOW THE LIMITATION OF IMPLIED WARRANTIES OR LIABILITY FOR INCIDENTAL, INDIRECT, SPECIAL, OR CONSEQUENTIAL DAMAGES, SO THE ABOVE LIMITATIONS MAY NOT ALWAYS APPLY. THE WARRANTIES IN THIS AGREEMENT GIVE YOU SPECIFIC LEGAL RIGHTS AND YOU MAY ALSO HAVE OTHER RIGHTS WHICH VARY IN ACCORDANCE WITH LOCAL LAW.

ACKNOWLEDGMENT

YOU ACKNOWLEDGE THAT YOU HAVE READ THIS AGREEMENT, UNDERSTAND IT, AND AGREE TO BE BOUND BY ITS TERMS AND CONDITIONS. YOU ALSO AGREE THAT THIS AGREEMENT IS THE COMPLETE AND EXCLUSIVE STATEMENT OF THE AGREEMENT BETWEEN YOU AND THE COMPANY AND SUPERSEDES ALL PROPOSALS OR PRIOR AGREEMENTS, ORAL, OR WRITTEN, AND ANY OTHER COMMUNICATIONS BETWEEN YOU AND THE COMPANY OR ANY REPRESENTATIVE OF THE COMPANY RELATING TO THE SUBJECT MATTER OF THIS AGREEMENT.

Should you have any questions concerning this Agreement or if you wish to contact the Company for any reason, please contact in writing at the address below.

Robin Short
Prentice Hall PTR
One Lake Street
Upper Saddle River, New Jersey 07458

About the CD

To install this software, place the CD into your CD-ROM drive. If you are using Windows, the Setup program should automatically start up (if it doesn't, just navigate to your CD drive under *My Computer* and double-click *Setup*). The Setup program will then guide you through the rest of the steps to install the software.

If you are using a Macintosh, just drag the *Printing Projects* folder onto your *Applications* folder on your hard drive.

In either case, you will need a minimum of 150 MB of free hard drive space to install all of these remarkable printing projects.

After you have installed the software, double-click the *Printing Projects* kitty icon (in Windows, a shortcut will be created on your desktop and a program group icon will appear under the Start/Programs menu) to run the program. *Please note: It may take a minute or two for the program to begin. Note, too, that the program runs off of your hard disk and you do not need the CD in your CD drive to run the program.*

The first time you run your *Printing Projects* program, it checks to see whether you already have Adobe Acrobat Reader installed. Acrobat Reader is needed to view and print all of the project files. If you don't already have it installed, your *Printing Projects* program will launch Adobe's (free) installer to allow you to install Acrobat Reader. If that is the case, you will need to re-launch *Printing Projects* after you finish installing Acrobat Reader, and the fun can then begin!

Using the program itself is very easy and intuitive. Just choose the project category you are interested in by clicking once on its icon. Submenus will appear to allow you to further refine your choice,

until you find just the project you are after. If you are confused at any step of the way, just look to the bottom of the screen where there will be a helpful hint to tell you what to do next. After you finally get a project open, you can print it by clicking on the Acrobat Reader printer icon (again, there is a hint in the program to show you how it looks). Some files have instructions included right in the project file. Some are more complex (such as iron-ons), and those will have separate (also printable) instructions. There are buttons for all such options along the top of the screen. One such button, the orange *Select a Project* button, opens a drop down menu that will allow you to select from different project variations or designs. Click on it to select a particular project.

Another button, the green *Helpful Products* button, suggests a few products that will help you create the project you are making. There's even a Web link there (in case you have Internet access) that takes you right to the Hewlett-Packard online store where you can shop for those products or other helpful printing products.

Also, there are *Back* and *Home* buttons that you can use to navigate back to a previous screen or to the home screen—just like a Web browser. Finally, use the *Exit* button to quit the program when you are finished.

It's all self explanatory, and LOTS of fun, so experiment, navigate, print, create, and have fun with *Printing Projects Made Fun & Easy.*

Technical Support: Prentice Hall does not offer technical support for this software. However, if there is a problem with the media, you may obtain a replacement copy by e-mailing us with your problem at: disc_exchange@prenhall.com.